Table of Contents

communication or written communication?

Question 20: If you were to ask your boss for a raise, what would be your reasoning?

Question 21: Are you willing to relocate or travel?

Question 22: What methods have you found to be successful in setting and achieving job objectives for your subordinates?

Question 23: No question at all.

Question 24: Would you ever lie for your company?

Question 25: Tell me about your current company's (profits, marketing plans, development projects, research methods, or other confidential matters).

Question 26: Don't you think you're overqualified for this position?

Question 27: Tell me about your persistence (analytical skills, creative problem solving, management ability, etc.).

Question 28: Tell me how you deal with angry or frustrated customers (employees, suppliers, etc.)

Question 29: Have you had much experience in firing employees?

Question 30: Tell me about a time something you did – or didn't do that you should have – that you now feel embarrassed about.

Question 31: Tell me about the strengths and weaknesses of your boss (company, executive management team, etc).

Question 32: Tell me about the most boring job you've ever had.

Question 33: How successful have you been in developing personnel?

Question 34: Are you applying for other jobs?

Question 35: What are your other career options at this point?

Question 36: Have you missed more than two days in a row (other than a scheduled vacation) in any of your previous positions?

Question 37: You seem to have changed jobs quite frequently. Why?

Question 38: What kind of person would you refuse to work with?

Question 39: Tell me about the most fun you've had on a job.

Question 40: What position do you prefer on a team working on a project?

Question 41: When I check your references, what will previous supervisors say your strongest point is?

Question 42: Give me an example of your initiative in a challenging situation.

Question 43: Tell me about the worst (job related) decision you ever made.

Question 44: Tell me about your dream job.

Question 45: Have you ever been asked to leave a position? or Have you ever been fired?

Question 46: If you were hiring someone for this job, what would YOU look for?

Question 47: What do you look for when you hire people?

Question 48: Are you a team player?

Question 49: Looking back on your career, do you think you've you done your best work?

Question 50: Explain how you would be an asset to this organization.

Question 51: What qualities do you look for in a boss?

Question 52: Tell me about a time when you helped resolve a dispute between others.

Question 53. How would you respond to your boss if he was in love with an idea that you thought was horrible?

Question 54: What have you done to improve your knowledge in the last year?

Question 55: What outside interests do you cultivate?

Question 56: Give me an example of a time when you were told "no."

Question 57: What do you do when a decision needs to be made, but no procedure exists?

Question 58: The "chink in your armor" question.

Question 59: Tell me about the last book you read.

Question 60: Tell me about a time you felt adequately recognized for a job well done.

Question 61: In what ways has your current boss contributed to your decision to search for another job?

Question 62: Can you recall a time when you or your team missed a deadline because no one realized it was a priority?

Question 63: Tell me about a time you used your enthusiasm to your advantage.

Question 64: Are you available to work nights and/or weekends?

Question 65: If you had the chance, what would you do differently in your life?

Question 66: You've been with your firm a long time. Won't it be difficult to switch to a new company?

Question 67. What do you see as the proper role/mission of:

Question 68: Why should I hire you from the outside when I could promote someone from within?

Question 69: Give me some examples of how your strengths compliment your boss's management style.

Question 70: Some people feel that staying at one job for so long demonstrates a lack of initiative. What's your take on that?

Question 71: Define [cooperation, management, team-building, marketing, operations, etc]

Question 72: How many projects can you handle at one time?

Question 73: What would you do if a co-worker wasn't pulling his/her weight …and was hurting your department?

Question 74: What problems do you experience in getting things done?

Question 75: How does your boss get the best out of you?

Question 76: How do you get the best out of your boss?

Question 77: What were your three most important responsibilities on your last job?

Question 78: When you managed others in previous positions, what was the average tenure of someone who resigned or quit to work elsewhere?

Question 79: What makes you angry?

Question 80: Have you ever experienced an employee or co-worker suddenly start acting out of character?

Question 81: All my other candidates have a college degree. Why should I hire you - considering you don't?

Question 82: Why aren't you earning more money at this stage in your career?

Question 83: Have you ever considered becoming an entrepreneur and starting your own company?

Question 84: What motivates you to do your best on the job?

Question 85: Can you explain your career progression from [position A] to [position B]? It appears to me that you took a step backwards. Is that true?

Question 86: What steps could you have taken to improve your career progress?

Question 87: What is more important to you: the money or the work?

Question 88: Have you ever been in a crisis situation where things got out of control? How did you handle it?

Question 89: Tell me how you plan your day/week/month.

Question 90: If it were offered to you, would you like to have your boss' job?

Question 91: Sell me this pen (pencil, stapler, adding machine, desk, clock, etc).

Question 92: Can you forget your education and start from scratch?

Question 93: Did you hold any budgetary responsibilities in your last position?

Question 94: What methods have you used in past performance reviews?

Question 95: Would you be willing to fill in for someone with lower-level responsibilities for an extended period of time?

Question 96: What has been the most expensive fiscal mistake of your career?

Question 97: Tell me how you organize and plan for major projects.

Question 98: The crazy question.

Question 99: Where do you see yourself six months (or one/five/ten years from now)?

Question 100: Do you have any questions for me?

Today's job market realities

It's estimated that today's workforce will change jobs at least seven times in their career and will change industries three times. However, those numbers are probably skewed low because they factor in the Baby Boom Generation which has shown a propensity for sticking with one or two jobs over a lifetime of work. What does this mean? Prepare to change jobs and even to change careers much more often than your parents. And knowing how to interview properly will help you change to the job you truly want at any particular stage of your life.

The best time to work on your career is when your job is secure. Even if you are happily employed today, you never know what will happen tomorrow. By practicing "Perpetual Career Management" – practicing the interview process, keeping your resume current, networking, updating your success stories, etc. - you will always be ready should a career disaster strike.

You're more than just a spoke in the wheel.

Work is a part of life, it's not life itself. You really don't owe it to any employer to dedicate your life to his benefit, though you would never imply anything like that. Don't sacrifice your family, community, church, recreation, or personal development for a job. A wise man once told me: If you are working more than 45 to 50 hours a week in your job, you're doing it wrong. You're limiting success in some other areas of your life and something just as important WILL suffer. Don't expect all your fulfillment, value, and meaning to com from the work you do.

It is critical that you develop a mindset of adaptability and a sense of how your contribution can benefit more than one company or organization because in today's fast paced world, your career path will most likely involve moving from company to company and industry to industry. Imagine climbing the portable rock wall at a state fair, or one that's set up in the mall. To reach the top, you'll have to move sideways and sometimes even back down, rather than just climbing the wall straight up. The irony is, climbing the ladder in only one organization will probably move you away from your strongest areas of competence as well as limit your earning potential. But by strategically changing companies you may be able to increase your income by 20 to 50 percent in one fell swoop. Have you heard of any one person getting such a raise while working at one company their entire career?

Before the interview

Before the interview, thoroughly research the company. This really matters. A lot. You have to know about the company's culture, its traditions, how the job is done, what success looks like, and what will be expected of you. Job candidates who wander in off the street with little knowledge of the company's needs are a complete waste of time for the interviewer. However, the candidate who knows the company's history, who the key players and key management personnel are, who knows why the position is open and can tailor his or her responses so that each answer to the interviewer's question meets the company's needs – that candidate is soon called an employee.

Next think about the job's published requirements and what the "unspoken" requirements might be (e.g. a sales rep should be self-secure, outgoing, while a retail assistant manager should be flexible, teachable, willing to go the distance) – using your list of personal characteristics as well as published requirements, create your personal punch list of traits/experience/education/expertise that the interviewer is looking for. Then articulate your own "must mention" punch list of things to bring up in the interview, to make sure you satisfy all of the interviewer's major items.

How can you
- Improve productivity
- Increase profit
- Increase sales
- Increase enjoyment
- Make life better
- Reduce costs
- Expand the market
- Increase market share
- Reduce shrinkage
- Improve quality
- Decrease down time
- Lower turnover

- Reduce time
- Create a new and better process
- Introduce new technology
- Create a better process
- Improve an existing process
- Reduce training time
- Enlarge a specific skill
- Create specific measures of performance
- Create new plans
- Implement a program
- Direct a program
- Solve a specific problem
- Identify solutions
- Foresee a need
- Achieve something new with less time, money, people, space, equipment
- Achieve same (or greater) results with fewer resources
- Accomplish more (or the same) with identical resources

An interview isn't about telling someone how great you are, but what YOU can do to make their business, operations, marketing, technology, or accounting …   better than it was before. Not about how great your product is, but how it can improve their business. Not about your education or experience, but about how you can use your education or experience to multiply their customers, increase market share, or boost their profits. A successful interview isn't about you; it's about your interviewer and what you can do for him.

The key to success in any interview is knowing what your interviewer needs, then pointing out how you, your experience, your education, your enthusiasm, your product, or your company can help meet those needs.

Next develop 2-3 TRUE stories you want to tell that pull together both lists, yours and the interviewer's. Write those stories on index cards and practice them until you can tell the stories fluently and convincingly. Record yourself on a video camera to see what the interviewer will see. Correct any flaws that jump out at you, then ask a friend, preferably one that will always tell you the truth, to watch the video and critique it. Ask this friend to NOT hold anything back (and don't get your feelings hurt either). You need this honesty so you can make improvements in your delivery.

Finally, at the interview use whatever questions come along to tell your well rehearsed stories. Always answer the question, but find a natural point to launch one of your stories. If you did your homework, those questions will be aligned with your stories. Weaving them in will seem natural.

Thee common areas you'll be able to weave in a story could stem from these types of questions:

> 1. Tell me about a time that you led a team.
> 2. Tell me about a time that you failed.
> 3. Tell me about a time that you dealt with an unproductive employee.

Don't fall for job market myths

1. If I can't find the right position for me, it probably doesn't exist

This is a typical, though inaccurate conclusion drawn by many frustrated job seekers. According to study after study, over 85% of all job vacancies are not available through traditional resources. The fact is managers and CEO's create positions for the right people every day.

THE TRUTH: Don't worry about a lack of available positions, concentrate instead on how to find what you really want and honing your interview skills.

2. I know how to position hunt

Most people position hunt with a resume, the traditional but ineffective method for finding a job. Consider this: standard resumes produce one inquiry for roughly every 85 resumes a company receives, but only half of those inquiries result in an interview. Since one interview takes place for every 170 resumes received and the average company conducts 10 interviews before making one offer, 1,699 resume senders are very disappointed.

THE TRUTH: Put old ideas behind you and learn to network.

3. I can always go to an employment agency

Of course you can, but remember that less than 7 percent of all professional, managerial, and executive positions are ever listed with agencies. One survey I read revealed that the average employment agency is able to set appointments for only one of every 20 candidates who contact them. The others just don't match their active position list.

THE TRUTH: Don't rely on traditional employment agencies for help since over 93 percent of the available top positions are not listed with them anyway.

4. A recruiter will actively market me to potential employers

That may have been true at some point in the past but today's reality is that the average recruiter is in the business of filling vacancies for companies. There is a big difference. As a position seeker, understand that companies pay big commissions (up to 50% of first year salary) to recruiters and that cash buys loyalty as well. Instead of marketing a candidate to the company, recruiters may try to fit an available worker into a vacant position.

THE TRUTH: If you aren't careful, a recruiter or job agency may try to manipulate you into a position you aren't looking for. If the recruiter starts "selling" you on a company or position, move on.

5. The Internet or the classifieds are where I should look

The Internet is a great resource for information, but if you've ever posted a position on one of the major job boards, you know how many resumes and application you get – thousands, sometimes tens of thousands. You may indeed find a position through the Internet, but chances are much better that there will be someone more qualified than you. If you desire a top position within a company, there is only a slim, tiny, miniscule chance the company is even looking to the Internet for an employee.

THE TRUTH: Answering ads and sending online applications is fine, but don't get your hopes up. Newspaper and Internet classifieds account for only a very small percentage of available positions so spend only a small amount of time here.

6. Employers have all the power

Ha-ha, umm, no. While it's true that employers have the power to hire and fire, they're as concerned with finding good employees as position seekers are about finding good positions. Recruiting and training costs are a major concern to all industries. Part of the problem is that many position seekers postpone position screening until after they're hired. Too many people find out their job ISN'T what they wanted only after working for a few months.

THE TRUTH: An employer needs you as much as you need him. Instead of going after a single position, run yourself a job campaign and pursue a number of offers. You are in the driver's seat.

7. The higher up I go, the more secure my position

This myth isn't even funny anymore. More than 500,000 middle managers and senior executives got the ax within the last few years and with the economy continuing to slide backwards despite Washington's failed efforts, they probably won't be alone. In fact, as you climb the ladder, you're held to a higher and higher standard as you become responsible for the actions of more and more people under you. It can truly be frightening.

THE TRUTH: Be prepared. Develop your job search strategy now before you have to create a plan B. This is a great idea even if your position seems secure today.

8. The best-qualified people always get the best positions

Not true. The people who get hired are the ones who first learn HOW to get hired … and then they practice and hone their skills.

THE TRUTH: The ones who get hired are the ones who know how to research their target company, uncover it's greatest needs and wants, and can adapt their skills and experience in such a way that the interviewer believes they are the answer to their prayers.

How to develop your own stories

People remember stories much better than raw facts. Without some good, memorable stories your candidacy with this position could be just another in a long list of qualified applicants. With a few highly memorable stories about how you solved problems in the past, you stand a much better chance of flipping a switch in your interviewer's mind that will make you a natural fit and your interview becomes more conversational and less like a traditional interview.

When you're crafting accounts of your successes, remember use the S.O.N.A.R. method to give them added punch.

S - situation.   Briefly explain the situation but don't spend too much time laying the background. Max time = 15 - 25 seconds.

O - opportunity.   Relate to the interviewer what the opportunity was and why it was important. Max time = 10 - 15 seconds.

N - next action.   Explain what you did, the actions you took and why you took them. Max time 45 - 60 seconds.

A - alternatives. Make certain the interviewer knows what alternatives you considered and how you may have adapted to any changes that arose during the process. Max time = 20 - 30 seconds.

R - results.   What happened? Make certain you can quantify your results in terms of verifiable, believable numbers. Max time = 10 - 15 seconds.

If you're having trouble coming up with positive stories about yourself or your work history, ask yourself these questions:

- Do I learn quickly? Are there examples of times when I learned something quickly?
- Has someone commented on how quickly I picked up on new information?
- Has anyone mentioned that I had a particular skill?
- Has anyone ever noticed that I had a way of dealing with situations effectively?
- Can I set something up or organize it efficiently?
- Whether it was a game, a party, a department, or just a new way of getting something done, was I able to organize it so that it did in fact get done as expected?

- Can I match people to their strengths?
- Have I ever advised anyone that they might be good at something, and it seemed to make sense to them?
- Have I ever assigned people to tasks that they felt were challenging and well suited to their abilities?
- Have I ever trained, developed, or motivated anyone?
- Have I ever trained, developed, or motivated anyone at work? In school? In a club or other social setting? On an athletic team or in some volunteer work?
- Have I ever trained, developed, or motivated my co-workers or family?
- Are there instances I can remember where I communicated clearly and accurately, so that people understood what I expected of them and what they could expect of me, and where this led to something getting done that needed doing?
- Am I a logical person who has figured out workable solutions to problems?
- Has anyone ever commented on that?
- Have I ever gotten people to interact with one another in harmony, in any sort of work or play?
- Have I ever pulled together a family project?
- Have I ever organized an amateur theater production? A work assignment?
- Have I ever coached or organized a sports team?
- Have I ever pulled together a volunteer effort?
- Have I ever organized a recreational pursuit such as a vacation, or building a small structure?
- Am I creative in some way?
- Have I ever produced anything that required some creativity?
- Have I written something creative?
- Have I ever drew or sculpted? Have I ever written a song or poem?
- Have I ever created a new outlook, or a new way to approach something?
- Have I put two ideas together in a way they hadn't been connected before?
- Have I ever figured out a way to solve a problem or find a new way of doing things?

- Did I ever think of a new game, or a new way of playing an old game?
- Can I recall instances where people acted in a way that showed they were happy to be working with me?
- Or where they told me directly that they liked to work with me?
- Or that they felt I brought a positive energy to the workplace?
- Do I have any special knowledge, talents, or experience?
- Do I have any special interests?
- Am I good with computers? With cars? With counseling?
- Do I know a lot about a particular market?
- Do I know a lot about a certain process, machine, or software?
- Do I know a lot about arranging travel?
- Do I have a knack for sales?
- Do I have a talent for producing something in a low cost way?
- Am I a prolific producer of anything?
- Do I write better than the average person?
- Do I understand compensation systems?
- Am I a good negotiator?
- Am I good at confronting people who need to be confronted?
- Am I good at diplomacy and tact when faced with an issue?
- Do I often tend to make people feel more confident, more peaceful, more invigorated?
- Have I ever brought enthusiasm to some activity?
- Have I ever gotten past a big obstacle? Turned around a difficult situation?
- Have I ever learned from a mistake?
- Have I ever made some changes that weren't easy?
- Have I ever achieved something that others recognized as requiring persistence and determination?
- In my own mind, can I see how my persistence might make me better able to relate to people, or give me credibility, or help me serve as a role model or set an example for someone?

Choose to look at the positive aspects of your personality and your abilities. Choose to look at the positives in your education, your experience, your achievements, and your future. Then match your most positive aspects to what you uncover as the company's most pressing need. Once you do this, make it one of your main bullet points when you're speaking with the interviewer or anyone else at the company.

A word about behavioral interviewing

Behavioral interviews are all the rage in human resources circles. Why? HR managers, unlike financial professional, believe the most accurate predictor of future performance is past performance under similar conditions. So, they want you to explain your career in a series of your own personal stories based on the situations they present. It can be a challenging exercise for the unprepared.

But preparing for a behavioral interview isn't difficult if you do a little research on the company and do a little reminiscing about your own work life. Does the company value planning and organizational skills? Think back to times when you've been responsible for planning a company or department project and what worked, what didn't, how it succeeded or failed, and what you learned (remember to use the S.O.N.A.R. method).

After you've determined which behavioral interview questions you might be asked during an   interview (see the chart below for examples), recall your own work experiences. Then design coherent stories around those personal situations.

These stories must be:
- True – never lie in an   interview. Facts presented in these situations are RARELY investigated but still ... never lie in an interview. There's too much risk.
- Detailed – and you better know the details inside and out. You'll be asked some questions by your interviewer.
- Brief and to the point – *never* ramble. Stay keenly aware of looks or actions on the part of your interviewer that could indicate boredom with your story.

These stories must have:
- A brief account of a *specific* challenge you faced.
- A brief account of the *specific* actions you took to conquer the challenge.
- A brief summary of the results (quantify these results with actual numbers).

Here are some areas where human resources managers might ask for your story and how they might ask it:

If the company values:	The interviewer or HR manager might ask:
Leadership	Tell me about a time you had to lead a team, what you did, and how did you handle any conflicts between members. Have others ever disagreed with your ideas? Tell me about it.
Performance	Tell me about a specific instance when you identified a problem. What did you do to solve it and what was successful in your approach? If you went to work for us today and we asked you to solve [X], what would be your first steps and why?
Decision Making	Tell me about a time when your use of good judgment made a difference. Have you ever had to make a quick decision before you could gather all the information you wanted? Tell me about what happened.
Interpersonal Skills	Tell me about a time you had to present an unpopular decision to your team. What was their response and how did you handle it? What did you learn from it? Have you ever disagreed with your boss or an upper management decision yet YOU had to implement it? How did that work?
Skill	Tell me about a particular time where you used [fill in the skill]. What was successful and unsuccessful about your approach? Can you [fill in required skill]? Tell me about a few instances when you used this skill.
Motivation	Tell me about a time you had to motivate a team. What methods did you use and why? Did those methods work? Why or why not? Tell me about a time when you had to go above and beyond the call of duty. What were the circumstances and what was the result?

Management	Tell me about a time when you had to discipline an employee. Without naming names, what were the circumstances and what steps did you take? How successful have you been at developing others? Give me some examples of how you trained an employee and where that employee is now.
Planning	Tell me how you prioritize your work or the work of others. Can you give me an example or two? What steps do you take in deciding to trust someone with developing a plan? Can you think of an instance when you've done this?
Customer Service	Tell me about the most irate customer you ever dealt with. What were the circumstances and what did you to resolve the situation? How do you satisfy a customer complaint without giving away the store? Give me an example of when you used just such an approach.

Remember these tips:

• Keep your answers short and succinct. Sixty seconds should be long enough for almost every question. Answers with stories using the S.O.N.A.R Method may take a little longer, but never more than three minutes.

• The best days to have an interview are Tuesday, Wednesday or Thursday. On Mondays everyone is dragging and on Fridays, they can't wait to get out of there.

• The best time to have your interview is between 8am and 10am. You **and** your interviewer will be sharper and your mind won't be cluttered with the day's events.

• Eighty-five percent of managers rank enthusiasm as the top characteristic they want in applicants. Smile! Give a firm handshake! Show some enthusiasm!

• Though the Internet has become the job seeker's venue of choice, less than 1% find work by responding to an Internet ad. Most job seekers find employment by networking with friends, neighbors, friends of parents, community organizations, recruiters, churches, former co-workers, former schoolmates, former co-workers, etc.

• Virtually NO interviewer has had any formal training in the craft. They rely solely on their gut instincts (bias) and previous experiences sitting on that side of the desk. Since you've prepared, you're in control.

If you admire someone for the success they've achieved, they probably didn't get there by being in the most lucrative industry, **but by doing work they generally enjoyed**. Don't be afraid to move to another career if you don't enjoy what you're doing for a living. Life's too short to hate your job for 40 years.

Use DISC To Your Advantage

DISC is a behavioral profiling language that is sometimes used to help with job candidate selection. It's a Four Factor model that has many uses and has been validated for decades as reliable. With a little training, you can use DISC to better understand your interviewer and tailor your responses to their behavioral preferences. In essence, you'll be speaking their language without their knowing it.

DISC stands for Dominance, Influence, Steadiness, and Cautiousness and while we all have a little of each in our own behavioral styles, there is generally one style that's more dominant than the others. The beauty of DISC is that it's all observable behaviors.

Dominance

Dominant behavioral styles are direct in their communications, sometimes quite blunt. They're results oriented, authoritative, strong-willed, decisive, can juggle many projects at once, and have a strong ego strength. They have a need to be in control and to direct. They are extroverted and will give their opinion willingly in clear specific language. They have a need for challenges and a strong desire to win. They will communicate in very certain terms if they disagree with you but will not hold a grudge if you disagree with them. They are very task oriented. Example could be Michael Jordan or even Mr. Smithers on *The Simpsons*.

People with a High D behavioral style love change and will initiate it, sometimes for no reason. You can recognize a High D by status symbols in their office: a picture with a political figure, trophies or awards, pictures with them as captain of the company softball team, or a prominent nameplate with their title. They will walk fast and be efficient (but not neat). They place high value on their time and they're very competitive.

If you notice these items, be brief in your answers. Get to the point quickly. Speak your mind and if they disagree with you, let them, but always give a friendly push back if your position is defensible by facts. Stick to business and don't worry with building a relationship at this stage of the interview process. Ask "What" questions and never ask a rhetorical or useless question.

Don't speculate but give accurate facts and figures. Provide opportunities for a win/win and never force them into a losing situation. Always refer to the results you've generated in previous positions.

Influencing

The Influencing behavioral style is everyone's friend. They are enthusiastic, trusting, charming, persuasive and talkative. They have a deep need to be liked and are highly optimistic on everything. A High I behavioral style will be involved in everything and they can tent to wear any emotions on their sleeve. High I's are extroverted and will consider the people perspective over the task perspective. Examples could include Robin Williams or Jimmy Fallon.

The High I behavioral style may not even notice change and they will naturally believe everything you tell them so it will be important to be honest and truthful. You'll know your in the office of a High I because it will generally be very disorganized and not very efficient. They may have an assistant who handles their lack of organization. They will use large sweeping gestures and may act more on impulse than other styles. They are very talkative and can be wordy. You may notice that they talk more in the interview than you do.

People with these behavioral traits are able to negotiate conflict and are generally team players. They will be verbally articulate and will focus on the "bright side" of any issue.

If you notice these traits, use your own enthusiasm to your advantage. Be excited about the opportunity (if you indeed are), and talk about the people you've helped, the customer's you've gotten to know, or the dreams you have for the position. Ask for their opinion and be fast, fun, and stimulating. Provide testimonials of your previous work habits, results, and experiences. Don't be tight lipped. Socialize with them, seek common friends or acquaintances, and always get everything in writing.

Steadiness

The Steady behavioral style is a relater. They are very relaxed, predictable, deliberate, and sincere. They can be incredibly patient and systematic. High S styles are great listeners but will be very undemonstrative in their emotions. They are introverted with a people orientation over a task orientation (similar to the High I). Examples could include Andy Griffith as Sheriff Taylor or Laura Bush.

Those with a High S behavioral style will resist change, especially change for change's sake. They generally need time to work through change and to adjust to it and their resistance may take a passive/aggressive stance. The more preparation for change you give to someone with a High S style, the better they like it. Why are they resistant? Because they are great planners and changes can disrupt plans. The great thing about these planners is they will finish what they start and will develop systems to get things accomplished.

If you notice that your interviewer is potentially a High S (and a large percentage of the populace is), rein in your gestures if you're given to using broad hand motions. Be aware of your body language and tone everything down. Talk a bit more softly and slowly and display as much patience and empathy as possible. Emphasize your desire for a loyal and long term relationship with your employer. Emphasize your desire to be a team player and support others on the team. Don't be loud, flashy, boisterous,talk about all the risks you've taken in past positions.

Cautious

The High C is analytical, precise, and very organized. This style has a deep seated need for procedures and will stick to known procedures and methods that have produced success in the past. They prefer to do everything by the book. The High C prefers to compete with themselves and is constantly striving for perfection, the "right" way of doing things. They would rather be conventional, conservative, and cautious than bold, daring, and brash. The lower their I score, the more tendency they will have toward perfectionism.

The High C is a data gatherer and is a tremendous asset to any team when trying to solve a problem or overcome a challenge. Their systematic way of thinking and attention to detail will cause them to ask clarifying questions and drive straight to the heart of an issue, though they can be highly diplomatic in how they do it.

If you believe your interviewer may be a High C, be prepared to offer proof
and evidence. Insure that your "ducks are all in a row" with anything you
present to them. Misspellings or poor grammar on a resume stands out to
them like a sore thumb so proofread everything ten times! Emphasize your
ability to follow company policy. Don't hesitate to make a direct point with
them so long as you have sufficient data and proof that you're right. They
won't chit-chat too much so insure that your answers are succinct, direct, to
the point, and accurate. They are very slow buyers and that may translate to
being very slow to hire … they are probably still processing data in their
minds.

Pulling it all together

Don't get caught up trying to read every action, phrase, gesture, body
language clue, or tonality of your interviewer but DO make a few mental
notes using the descriptions above. Very few people in the population are a
pure style (only one dominating DISC style) but most people are a blend of
different styles.

Beware of other behavioral models that try to classify people into one of only
16 different styles. Though you can potentially glean some information from
those approaches, each person is too unique to classify into only one of 16
types. Studies have shown that 53% of the population fits into one of those
types but what about the other 47%? Using such a limiting evaluation is
about like flipping a coin.

Use what you've learned as an indicator, not as a rule. Use it to make a
stronger connection with your interviewer and to adapt how you
communicate so that your message isn't lost in translation.

Do Your Due Diligence

Today, getting the interview in the first place is an achievement. You've survived the automated keyword review of your resume by an online artificial intelligence algorithm, you've passed the scrutiny of an executive assistant, got passed several HR people at varying levels, and probably a recruiter.

Don't blow it by not being prepared.

The moment you learn you've been selected for an interview, the clock starts ticking and the onus is on you to know more about the company, its history, its present, and its future than ever before. You need to know how they go to market, what their strategies are, how they measure success, and what analysts are saying.

You'll need to pull company financial reports, understand the organizational chart, and understand their social media strategy. You need to read everything your can possibly find on their executive team and your interviewer.

If you're interviewing for a marketing position, you'll need to know their marketing strategies and tactics. If you're interviewing for an IT slot, you'll need to know what software they use and any programming languages you'll have to know (or learn). If you're interviewing for an operations position, you'll need to know the company's operational tactics and methods of execution.

You'll need to know this company inside and out because chances are very good your competitors (other job applicants) will know it too.

Another significant part of your due diligence is to utilize social media to see if you have any contacts within the company. Engage your contacts and ask for help. Tell them what you've learned about the company and ask if you're on track. Ask for introductions to key players within the company if you're using LinkedIn. Follow their "likes" and read everything they write or comment about.

The more data you have on your target company, the more you'll seem like an insider and the interviewer will interpret it as passion for the company and its mission.

The Top 100 Interview Questions

Question 1: Tell me about yourself.

Not really a question is it? The real question is "who are you?" This "question" occurs in more than 80 percent of all interviews and is the most common lead off question. It seems so natural, like it was just a part of a conversation but this question is far from innocent. Have a short statement prepared in your mind but be careful that it doesn't sound rehearsed and limit it to work-related items only. Talk about things you have done and jobs you have held that relate to the position you are interviewing for. Start with the item farthest back and work up to the present, and use this opportunity to highlight why YOU are the best candidate for the position.

WORST ANSWER: Many job candidates, unprepared for the question, skewer themselves by starting with the past, rambling, recapping their life story, delving into ancient work history or personal matters. Trust me, the interviewer does not care!

BEST ANSWER: Forget the past for right now and tell the interviewer why you are well-qualified for the position. Remember: the key to all successful job interviewing is matching your qualifications to the company's and the interviewer's needs. You gotta sell what the buyer is buying. This is the single most important strategy in job hunting, interviewing, and landing the position you want.

So, before you answer this or any question it's critical to uncover your interviewer's greatest need, want, problem, or goal. To do this, take these two steps:

- Do your homework *before* the interview to uncover the interviewer's wants and needs, not the generalized needs of the company or even of the   industry.
- Early the interview, perhaps even before it gets fully underway, ask for a more complete description of what the position involves.   You might say: "I do have a list of achievements I'd like to talk with you about, to make the best use of our time together, I'd like to talk directly to your needs. To help me do that, could you tell me more about the most important priorities of this position?   All I really know is what I

(heard from the recruiter, read in the classified ad, etc.)"

Then, ALWAYS follow-up with a second question and possibly, third or fourth, to draw out his needs even more. Surprisingly, it's usually this second or third or fourth question that reveals what the interviewer is *most* looking for.

How to do this? Ask. "And in addition to that ...?" or, "Is there anything else you see as essential to success in this position?" or "What else? Is there something else you're thinking of?" or "Would you mind elaborating on that?" or even something as simple as "Tell me more."

This process will not feel easy or natural at first, because it is easier to simply answer the questions, but if you uncover the employer's wants and needs your answers will ironically make the most sense. And hiring YOU will make the most sense. Practice asking these key questions before giving your answers, the process will feel more natural and you will be light years ahead of the other job candidates you're competing against.

After discovering what the interviewer is looking for, explain how the needs of this job align with tasks you've succeeded at before. Give him several examples, but make sure he sees the striking parallels between what he needs and what you've already done. Be sure to illustrate with specific examples your responsibilities and especially your achievements, all of which are geared to present yourself as a perfect match for the needs just described.

Question 2: What are your greatest strengths?

I don't like this question and have a hard time understanding its repeated use (perhaps it's because most interviewers don't know what else to ask). It seems like a softball, "Larry King" type question, but it can still knock you back if you're unprepared.

WORST ANSWER: Sappy humility is no better than blatant overconfidence. Above all, don't stall. And make sure the strengths you list are different. Honesty, telling the truth and integrity are all the same thing – that counts as ONE strength!

BEST ANSWER: Since your first key strategy is to uncover your interviewer's highest wants and needs before you answer any question, THAT has to be your template. And, you now know how to do this after reading Question One, above.

Before the interview, prepare a list of your three greatest strengths with specific examples to illustrate each, and add "proof" from one of your recent and most impressive achievements. This list of strengths with examples from your achievements should be so well committed to memory that you can recite them perfectly after being shaken awake at four in the morning. Then, once you uncover your interviewer's greatest wants and needs, you can choose those achievements from your list that best match up.

Generally speaking, the 10 most desirable traits that great employers desire in their employees are:

1. A record of achievements that match well with the employer's greatest wants and needs.
2. Intelligence and business "savvy".
3. Honesty, integrity, decency.
4. A team player who meshes well with interviewer's team and can integrate with the company's culture.
5. Likability, a positive attitude, and *maybe* a sense of humor. Be careful here, the wrong humor can get you in trouble.
6. Excellent communication skills.
7. Dedication and a willingness to go the extra mile to achieve excellence.
8. A goal setter with a clear sense of purpose.
9. A high level of motivation and the enthusiasm to back it up.
10. Confidence.

Companies on the downswing will SAY they value these same things, but will consistently fail to hire employees who exemplify these traits. As a result, those companies will have a high turnover rate, unhappy employees, a focus on policies not principles, a belief that employees are lazy and untrustworthy, an obsession with today rather than tomorrow, and leadership in all the wrong places ... but that's another eBook.

Question 3: What are your greatest weaknesses?

Beware - this is an "eliminator question," designed to shorten the list of candidates. Any confession of a weakness or fault will earn you an "A" for honesty, but an "F" for the interview.

WORST ANSWER: A weak or half-hearted attempt to disguise a strength as a weakness.

> *Example: "I sometimes push my people too hard. I like to work with a sense of urgency and everyone is not always on the same wavelength."*

Ugh! What a load of bologna. Interviewers see right through it, and though better than admitting a flaw outright, it's too widely used and makes you look over-coached and unnatural.

BEST ANSWER: Assure the interviewer that you can think of nothing that would stand in the way of your performing in this position with excellence. Then, quickly review your strongest qualifications and how they match with the interviewer's needs, which is easy if you've already uncovered those needs.

> *Example: "No one is perfect, but based on what you've told me about this position, I firmly believe I'm an outstanding match. What I believe you're concerned with can be summed up with two things: One, do I have the qualifications to do the job well and, two, do I have the motivation to do it well? Everything in my background shows I have both the qualifications and a strong desire to achieve excellence in whatever I take on. So I can say in all honesty that I see nothing that would cause you even a small concern about my ability or my strong desire to perform this job with the excellence this company expects from ALL employees."*

An alternate strategy (if you don't yet know enough about the position to talk about such a perfect fit), is to describe what you like most and like least, making sure that what you like most matches up with the most important qualification for success in the position, and what you like least is not essential.

> *Example: Let's say you're applying for a teaching position. "If given a choice, I like to spend as much time as possible in front of my students teaching, as opposed to grading papers and filing reports. Of course, I long ago learned the importance of filing paperwork properly, and I do*

it conscientiously. But what I really love to do is teach.

This example could easily be adapted to a management position or a sales position. Few people love paperwork. You can use that almost universal disdain to your advantage should the question be presented to you in your interview.

Question 4: Why are you leaving (or did you leave) your current (or former) position?

Interviewers are looking for potential problems and this question could reveal your impatience, lack of respect for authority, job-hopping tendencies, or any one of a host of issues. You best be prepared for this question since it is almost always asked in some form by interviewers. No matter what, never go negative about a former (or current) position, a boss, or any other situation that had a negative effect on you or your career. Few things can sour an interview more than going negative – even if it was warranted – so steer clear of the temptation.

WORST ANSWER: Speaking badly of your previous industry, company, board, boss, staff, employees, co-workers, or customers. This rule is written in stone: *never go negative.* Any mud you sling will get your own hands dirty and the interviewer will see it. Especially avoid words like "personality clash", "couldn't get along", "butted heads" or others that could cast a long, dismal shadow on your competence, integrity, or temperament.

BEST ANSWER:
(If you have a job currently)
If you're not quite 100% committed to leaving your current job, say so. There's absolutely nothing wrong with that and it will put you in a much stronger position. But don't be coy or play hard to get either. Be honest and tell the interviewer what you're hoping to find in a new spot. Of course, as stated often before, your answer will be all the stronger if you have already uncovered what this position is all about and you match your desires and abilities to it.

(If you do not currently have a job)
Be honest, but be wary. The best reasons for leaving a position include:
- The opportunity to increase your income

- Moving to an area with family
- The chance to move to a position of more authority and responsibility
- The prospect of moving to a position with more opportunities for professional growth

No matter what, never lie about having been fired. Not only is it unethical to lie, it's too easily checked and found out. More and more companies are finally seeing the light and performing those reference and background checks, so make certain you never lie about being fired. You can, however, try to deflect the reason from you personally if your firing was the result of a takeover, merger, division wide layoff, or reduction in force (RIF).

For all prior positions: Make sure you've prepared a brief reason for leaving. Best reasons: more money, opportunity, responsibility or growth.

Question 5: What are your career goals?

Interviewers want to see that you have goals you're working towards and that you understand long range planning. They may also be trying to take the pulse of your personal ambition. If you're too specific, i.e., naming the promotions you someday hope to achieve, you'll sound presumptuous. If you're too vague, you'll seem directionless. Having no answer makes you sound like a moron.

WORST ANSWERS:

1. Too much ambition or impatience with how career progression actually works.

> *Example: Assume you're applying for a management position – never say anything like: "I want your job. I plan to be promoted to middle management within 2 years and senior management shortly thereafter with potential for a seat on the board of directors within 10 years ... MAX." – yes, I've been told this exact thing by an interviewee!*

2. Having no goals or ambition whatsoever – a "I'm not really sure I've thought that much about it" answer. Yes, I've actually heard that one, too.

Another reason an interviewer may ask this question is to see if you're settling for this position and using it merely as a stopover until something better comes along.

BEST ANSWER: Reassure your interviewer that you're looking to make a long-term commitment … that this position entails exactly what you want to do and what you can do extremely well. As for your future, you believe that if you perform each job at hand with excellence, future opportunities will take care of themselves. Not a hands off approach per se, but a willingness to trust in yourself and that what you do will speak for itself

> *Example: "I am definitely interested in making a long-term commitment to my next position. Judging by what you've told me about this position, it's exactly what I'm looking for and what I am very well qualified to do. In terms of my future career path, I'm confident that if I do my work with excellence, opportunities will inevitably open up for me. It's always been that way in my career, and I'm confident I'll have similar opportunities here."*

Question 6: Why should we hire you?

If you don't know why, should the interviewer know why? You have to partner the interviewer's needs with what you can do for him. That will be the recurring theme throughout this entire book.   Believe it or not, this is a killer question because so many candidates are unprepared for it. If you stammer or ad-lib you've blown it.

WORST ANSWER: Having no answer or stalling while you think about it. If you're being interviewed by a committee, trust me, one of the interviewers is kicking another under the table as they muse at your inability to convince them you're worth hiring.

BEST ANSWER: Hopefully, I've been able by now to convince you of the critical nature of uncovering your interviewer's needs before you answer a single question. Despite the jarring nature of this question, knowing the employer's greatest needs and desires will give you a big leg up over other candidates because you will give him better reasons for hiring you than anyone else is likely to … reasons related directly to his needs.

It really doesn't matter whether your interviewer asks you this question – this**is arguably the most important question of your interview because he must answer it favorably in his own mind before you will be hired.** <u>So</u>

<u>help him out!</u>   Lead the interviewer through each of the position's requirements as you understand them and as they have been communicated to you, and follow each one with a reason why you meet that requirement better than anyone.

Every one of these duos (his needs matched by your qualifications) is a home run that drives up your personal score. It is your best opportunity to outshine your competition and get to work as quickly as possible.

Question 7: Why do you want to work at our company?

You *better* know why because this question tests whether you've done any homework about the firm. It's time to read the chairman's letter to shareholders, read the annual report, and use Google or Yahoo! Finance to dig up anything interesting. If you haven't taken a few minutes to do these simple things, you lose. If you have, you win big.

WORST ANSWER: Anything to do with pay, or a stammering, stuttering answer that is really vague, or an answer that focuses on yourself.

BEST ANSWER: Answers could include work/life balance, the stellar reputation of the company, the desire to be part of a great tradition, the company's history of innovation, or any other positive (but true) things you've learned about the company. Use your network to uncover something great about the company, and then weave that story into your answer.

> *Example: "I know that this company allows the use of its private jet to fly cancer patients to St. Jude's Children's Research Hospital when those children need a flight to Memphis. That impressed me. I want to work for a company that values people and uses its resources to make someone's life better."*

> *"You value creativity and innovation. I've heard that researchers are encouraged to spend at least two hours each day trying to uncover ways to improve your existing product line. I want to work for a company that doesn't box people in and that stimulates creativity in its employees."*

This question is your opportunity to hit a home-run, thanks to the in-depth research you've done before the interview. The best sources for researching your target company are annual reports, the corporate newsletter, and contacts you know at the company. Don't overlook the company's suppliers, advertisements, articles about the company in the trade press, Google, or your personal network.

Question 8: What are you looking for in your next job/company/position?

This isn't just an extension of Question 7; it asks what *you* are looking for, not what aspect of the interviewer's company interests you; however you have the opportunity to pair up this company's strengths with your own.   This is occasionally asked by an experienced interviewer who thinks you may be overqualified, but knows better than to show his hand by posing his objection directly. So he'll use this question instead, which often gets a candidate to reveal that, indeed, he or she is looking for something other than the position at hand.

WORST ANSWER: Anything that indicates you don't understand what the position entails or otherwise shows your lack of research.

BEST ANSWER: The best answer is to describe what this company is offering, making sure your answer is believable. How? Use specific reasons, stated with sincerity, why each quality represented by this opportunity is attractive to you and matches your prior achievements and strengths.

> *Side Note: If you're coming from a company that's a leader in the field (or admired or glamorous), your interviewer(s) may feel that his own company is inferior or inadequate. They may feel a bit defensive about being "second best" to the company you're coming from, worried that you may consider them a step down from your current company. This anxiety could well be there even though you've done nothing to cause it. It's up to you to alleviate this anxiety by putting their values high on the list of exactly what you're looking for, providing credible reason for wanting these qualities. If you don't answer this inadequacy complex with genuine enthusiasm for the firm, its culture, location, industry, etc, you'll leave the interviewer suspecting that a hot shot like you, coming from a big shot company, just couldn't be happy at an*

unknown manufacturer based in Wichita, Kansas. And no one wants unhappy workers.

Question 9: Why have you been out of work so long? or Why WERE you out of work so long (before accepting a previous position)?

This question is designed to jar you. Surely no one would ask THAT question would they? Your interviewer might, if it applies, ask you this question. Of course, your answer should be honest. If you were finishing a degree, getting more training on your own, or taking some time to care for a sick relative, assure the interviewer that these are finished and that you're very serious about this open position. But again, tailor your responses to the interviewer's needs.

Be very careful how you respond.   You don't want to seem like damaged goods that no one else wants. If you've had several interviews with no callbacks of offers, PLEASE don't bring this up. Even if you're a perfect match, there will be some lingering doubt in the interviewer's mind. They will wonder what's wrong and if other companies have uncovered something unsavory about you.

WORST ANSWER: "I've been hanging out (on the beach and at the ski resorts, searching for a job the last 12 months)." Another bad answer is "I'm not sure ..." or resorting to whining about the unfairness of the economy, Congress, the President's policies, people in the industry, etc.

BEST ANSWER: You want to emphasize factors which have prolonged your job search   **by your own choice**.

> *Example: "After my job was downsized, I made a conscious decision that I wouldn't jump at the first opportunities to come along, and there were a few that DID. I wanted to think through this process and make a more deliberate decision. In my life, I've found out that you can always turn a negative into a positive IF you try hard enough. This is what I determined to do. I decided to think through what I do best, what I most want to do, where I'd like to do it...and then identify those companies that could offer such an opportunity. That's why I'm here*

today."

Or try this approach:

> *"In all honesty, I believe we have to factor in the recession (consolidation, stabilization, etc.) in the (banking, financial services, manufacturing, advertising, etc.) industry and I've decided to be very selective in the company I choose to work for. I want a strong, well run company that I can be proud of and where I can make a real contribution over the long haul. So between my being selective and the companies in our industry downsizing, the process has taken time. But in the end, I'm convinced that when I do find the right match, all that careful evaluation from both sides of the desk will have been well worth it for both the company that hires me."*

Interviewers are keenly interested in making certain they don't make a bad hire. It taints their standing and makes them look incompetent. If you place the slightest doubt in the interviewer's mind about your fitness for a position by indirectly mentioning that "no one else wants me," your chances are slim; however, if you appear to be a candidate that is in control of his emotions and one that doesn't make hasty decisions, your total score will rise in the interviewer's mind.

Question 10: Tell me about a time your work was criticized.

This is a tricky question. Answer it on its face value and you've inadvertently admitted a weakness, but you can't dodge it by pretending you've never been criticized. Who hasn't been criticized? Yet admitting potential faults and failures that you'd just as soon forget can be damaging to your chances for getting the job offer.

But not all interviewers are trying to get you to admit a weakness. Some may be trying to gauge   how well you accept criticism and direction, both highly desirable traits in employees.

WORST ANSWER: Any answer that reveals inner bitterness, shifts blame, flips the criticism back on your boss, or otherwise makes you appear weak.

BEST ANSWER: Begin by emphasizing the extremely positive feedback you've gotten throughout your career and (if it's true) that your performance reviews have been uniformly excellent.

> *Example: "My career has been marked by a lot of positive feedback from my superiors and it shows on my performance reviews. If I'm pressed to come up with a criticism, hmm, you know, nothing really comes to mind immediately but I can think of several instances where I've been coached and mentored [cite examples if possible]. Those were some extremely valuable times in my life because they helped me grow professionally and personally."*

We all know no one is perfect and as a mature employee, you always welcome suggestions on how to improve your performance. Then, you might give an example of a minor learning experience from early in your career and relate the ways this lesson has since helped you. This demonstrates that you learned from the experience and the lesson is now one of your stronger characteristics.

If you are pressed for an example of criticism from a recently held position, choose something fairly trivial that in no way is essential to your successful performance. Add that you've learned from this, too, and over the past several years/months, it's no longer an area of concern because you now make it a regular practice to use what you learned to correct that aspect of your work.

Another way to answer this question would be to describe your intention to broaden your mastery of an area of growing importance in your field. For example, this might be a computer program you've been meaning to sit down and learn… a new management technique you've read about…or perhaps attending a seminar on some cutting-edge branch of your profession.

Again, the key is to focus on something not essential to your brilliant performance but which adds yet another dimension to your already impressive knowledge base.

Question 11: Can you work under stress?

This is a *SURPRISE!* question most of the time because it's asked after some joviality or small talk. It should be an easy question, but you want to make your answer believable.

WORST ANSWER: Stammering or stuttering, and   murmuring a weak reply.

BEST ANSWER: Of course! Then prove it with a vivid example of a goal or project you accomplished under pressure.

I was personally asked this question several years ago when interviewing for an upper management position. My answer to the CEO was, "What kind of stress?" He was intrigued. "What do you mean?" he asked, his brow furrowed. "There are two kinds: the kind when you're making money and the kind when you're not. Although I certainly DO have a preference, yes, I can work under all sorts of stress," I replied smiling. I eventually got the job because I explained the difference between having too much business versus the stress of not having enough (and wondering how you're going to make payroll – yeah, THAT'S stress).

Question 12: What changes would you implement if we hired you today?

Watch out! This question can derail your candidacy faster than a bomb on the tracks – and just as you are about to be hired.   No matter how bright you are, you cannot know the right actions to take in a position before you settle in and get to know the operation's strengths, weaknesses key people, financial condition, methods of operation, etc. If you lunge at this temptingly baited question, you will probably be seen as someone who shoots from the hip. Moreover, no matter how comfortable you may feel with your interviewer, you are still an outsider. No one, including your interviewer, likes to think that a know-it-all outsider is going to come in, turn the place upside down and with sweeping, grand gestures, promptly demonstrate what jerks everybody's been for years.

WORST ANSWER: Almost anything you could say.

BEST ANSWER: You want to take a good hard look at everything the company is doing before making any recommendations.

> *Example: "Well, just like a good doctor only gives a diagnosis after an examination, I'd need some time to understand your operation (no pun*

intended). Should you hire me, as I hope you will, I'd want to take a good hard look at everything you're doing and understand why it's being done that way. I'd like to have in-depth meetings with you and the other key people to get a deeper grasp of what you feel you're doing right and what could be improved.

"From what you've told me so far, the areas of greatest concern to you are…" (name them. Then do two things. First, ask if these are in fact his major concerns. If so then reaffirm how your experience in meeting similar needs elsewhere might prove very helpful).

No intelligent interviewer wants to hire someone to start a new job with guns blazin'. That's a recipe for creating enemies for the interviewer. You'd much rather come across as cool and collected, a careful analyzer and evaluator who makes the best possible decision.

Question 13: What salary do you need to cover your expenses?

Never fall for this question. First, it's a bit condescending to ask what your monthly expenses may be. Second, you're obviously hoping that your salary will cover much more than just your expenses. Third, always remember the golden rule of negotiating: **whoever mentions the first number loses.**
If forced, give your desired salary range instead of an amount equal to your expenses.

WORST ANSWER: Anything that includes a number.

BEST ANSWER: "That's an interesting question. I know what the ranges are at other companies but I'd be curious to know the normal salary range for this position."

This is a loaded question and, in my opinion, a nasty little game that you will probably lose if you answer first. So, don't answer it. In most cases, the interviewer, taken off guard, will tell you what the range is. If not, say that it can depend on the details of the job. ONLY IF YOU'RE PRESSED, give a ridiculously wide range "based on your research" with the lower number being what you really hope for.

Example: "I'm really not comfortable discussing salary expectations at this point, but from the research I've conducted, I know that others in this industry pay their [insert name of position]'s anywhere from $55,000 to $137,500 plus benefits. As long as you're in that range, I think we will probably be able to work something out should we both decide this is a fit ... and I hope that we both do!"

Question 14: What salary are you worth? or What salary expectations do you have?

This one isn't quite as offensive! Believe it or not, this question comes up surprisingly early in many interviews. Interviewers want to weed out early those who's expectations are way out of line.   This is your most important negotiation. Handle it wrong and you can blow the job offer or start work at far less than what the company was willing to pay.

WORST ANSWER: Again, anything with a number.

BEST ANSWER: To gain your maximum salary negotiating power, remember these guidelines:

1. Never initiate the salary question. Make the interviewer do it first. Good salespeople sell their products before talking price. GREAT salespeople ask the prospect what they think the product is worth. So should you. By tailoring your stories so that your abilities and experiences match the interviewer's needs, you'll make the interviewer want you first and reveal what he's able to offer. Your bargaining position meanwhile will become much stronger.

2. If the interviewer starts talking salary too early (you'll know), postpone the question, saying something like, "Money is important to me, but isn't my main concern. Opportunity and growth are far more important. What I'd rather do, if you don't mind, is explore if I'm right for the position, and then talk about money. Would that be okay?" You have to have enough time to create the desire for your qualifications.

3. The inviolable rule of every negotiation is   the side with the most information wins.   After you've sold the interviewer on your qualifications and it's time to talk salary, your goal is to get the employer talking about what *he's* willing to pay before you reveal what *you're* willing to accept. So, when asked about salary, respond by asking, "I'm sure the company has already established a salary range for this position. Could you tell me what that is?" Or, "I want an income commensurate with my ability and qualifications. I trust you'll be fair with me. Or, take the direct route, "What does this position pay?" Some negotiators will recognize what you're doing and balk at giving you a figure. At this point, feel free to say that you've done plenty of research and you know what the position is worth as well as the "upgraded options" you bring to the table. But never, ever, ever be the first to say a number.

4. Know how low you're willing to go. To know what's reasonable, research the job market in general and this position specifically for any pertinent salary information. Remember that most managers and executives seek at least a 20-25%$ pay hike when they switch jobs. If already you're grossly underpaid, you may want more.

5. Never lie about what you currently make (it's too easily verified), but feel free to include the estimated cost of all your benefits, which could well tack on 25-50% more to your present "cash-only" salary.

For a great book on salary negotiating, read Roger Dawson's <u>Secrets of Power Salary Negotiating.</u>

Question 15: How long would you expect to work for us if we hire you?

Specifics here are not good. Never fall for a trap like this. Many times your interviewer will ask this question after seeing that you've changed jobs on a regular basis (say every three years). They are legitimately concerned that you'll have a three year shelf life and then jump ship after they've invested time, effort, and money in training you.

WORST ANSWER: Anything specific like, "I plan to work 5 to 10 years." or "As long as I'm not bored."

BEST ANSWER: Assure the interviewer that you're looking for a long term relationship and that you haven't thought about when you might quit a job you don't already have! Depending on the tone in your interview, you might answer a question with a question, "If you hire me, how long do you anticipate keeping me?" And then smile really big.

Question 16: What are your thoughts on reporting to a younger person (minority, woman, man, etc)?

Though it truly is a shame that some interviewers feel the need to ask this question, many understand the reality of prejudice in the workplace. Most savvy interviewers feel it's better to uncover these prejudices out beforehand. The real trap this question presents is that in today's environment, even a well thought out answer can plant your foot squarely in your mouth! Avoid anything which smacks of a patronizing or an insensitive attitude, such as "I think they make terrific bosses" or "Hey, some of my best friends are …"

Since your interviewer knows that anyone with an IQ higher than their shoe size will at least try to answer this question correctly, he will primarily be evaluating your sincerity.. "Does he or she really feel that way?" is what the interviewer will be wondering. So make your answer believable and not just automatic. If the firm is wise enough to have promoted people on the basis of ability alone, they're most likely proud of it (justifiably), and wish to hire others who will wholeheartedly share that strong sense of fair play.

WORST ANSWER: Stammering, asking him to repeat the question, or sounding canned.

BEST ANSWER: You greatly admire any company that hires and promotes on merit alone and you   couldn't agree more with that philosophy. The age (gender, race, etc.) of the person you report to would certainly make no difference to you.

> *Example: "I'd be honored to work here, quite frankly, and no matter who I report to, I can assure you that person will have my respect and loyalty. I'd be proud to work for any company that can see past petty prejudices and promote people on the basis of merit and I'd be excited to know that same opportunity was afforded to me."*

Whoever has that position has obviously earned it and knows their job well. Both the person and the position are fully deserving of respect. You believe that all people in a company, from the receptionist to the Chairman, work best when their abilities, efforts and feelings are respected and rewarded fairly, and that includes you. That's the best type of work environment you can hope to find.

Question 17: I'm just a little bit concerned you don't have the experience or qualifications we consider ideal.

Though this appears as a statement, it really is a question, candidate and it has the potential to be a make-or-break question. The interviewer is asking you to convince him that you're the right If you find yourself facing this statement/question, there's a great chance that the interviewer likes what he sees, but has doubts over one important area. If you can reassure him on this point, the job could be yours.   The concern is usually not that you are totally missing a certain qualification, such as the CPA certification, but rather that your experience is light in one key area. You certainly wouldn't apply for a position that required a CPA certification if you didn't have it. Before any interview, identify *your* weakest points from *this* company's viewpoint. Then prepare the best answer you possible can to shore up your defenses. To overcome this question, rely on your master strategy of uncovering the employer's greatest wants and needs and then matching them with your strengths. Since you already know how to do this from Question 1, you are in a much stronger position.

WORST ANSWER: Jumping on the defensive or getting your feelings hurt.

BEST ANSWER: Re-emphasizing your strong points and how they match with your interviewer's greatest needs. When the interviewer does present this objection, you should:

> 1. Accept and agree with him on the importance of this qualification.
> 2. Explain how your other strengths indicate an ability to overcome your lack of expertise in this area.
> 3. When taken as a package, you believe your strengths make you strong candidate. It's really your combination of qualifications that's most important.

Then review the areas of your greatest strengths that match up most favorably with the company's most urgent wants and needs. This is powerful way to handle this question for two reasons. One, while you are giving your interviewer more ammunition in the his area of concern, you're shifting his focus away from this one, isolated area and putting it on the unique combination of strengths you offer, strengths which tie in perfectly with his greatest needs.

Question 18: What were your three most important responsibilities in your last job?

This is a simple, information gathering question. The interviewer's motive behind asking it is understanding your functional background and gaining a depth of understanding about how you've been trained, what you understood about your previous position, and whether your previous employer invested any effort in training you. This question also gives you the opportunity to match your previous experiences with what you've uncovered as the interviewer's greatest needs.

WORST ANSWER: Vague generalities, or unimportant tasks that anyone with a pulse could do. "I made out the schedule for three people" won't cut it.

BEST ANSWER: Tying your abilities to this company's needs. If the company needs an organizer you would emphasize your responsibilities in previous positions related to organization. If the company needs a communicator, your responsibilities should indicate your responsibilities and abilities to communicate. Remember Question 2?

> *Example: "In my previous position I was an area manager at a home improvement retailer with leadership responsibilities for 12 associates, so obviously leadership by example was a very important responsibility. I was also responsible for communicating home office directives to my team. I learned early on the importance of NOT sugar coating those communications but getting information to the team as quickly as possible so we could stay on track. I would also rank team building as a very important responsibility. Without a cohesive team that could pull together at a moments notice under a strong leader, we wouldn't have accomplished the consistent sales and profit increases that we did."*

Question 19: What was more important in your

previous positions, oral communication or written communication?

The higher up the professional ladder you climb, the more important written communication will become. Most business decisions DO begin with spoken communications but any instruction or communication, whether within the company or without, needs to be followed up and enforced in writing. The interviewer may be trying to see the positions you've held previously are of a higher level or just words on paper.

WORST ANSWER: Any "pat" answer that indicates you don't understand the importance of this particular question.

BEST ANSWER: If you indicate that many of your instructions (both going out and coming in) were initially begun as oral, but you took the opportunity to convert them to written communications to insure clarity, you'll shine. Obviously you don't want to come across as being afraid of your own shadow and afraid to make a decision without someone's "signing off" on it, but when it came to decisions of importance, you wanted to make sure everyone was on the same page.

> *Example: "Many, if not most, communications began with a conversation, either in the hallway, in an office, or in a meeting, so oral communication was highly important in my previous position. That being said, depending on the importance of the communication, I regularly took the time to insure all concerned were on the same page, so I would initiate a memo to confirm what was discussed, the time frame, who the responsible parties were, and what success looked like. When I would attend a seminar or meeting, I would regularly synthesize my notes and report back to my boss so she could see what I learned and know what was going on. Oral communication is highly important in any position, but follow-up and enforcement usually require some form of written communication."*

Note also that the smaller the firm, the more it will rely on verbal communications. The larger the firm, the more it will rely on written communications. Beware of showing too much formality if you've only worked for smaller firms and too much informality if you've only worked for larger firms. Interviewers are on the lookout for line managers who prefer memos and written communications over personal contact. It could signify a lack of people skills unless memos were needed to confirm or reinforce previous communications.

Question 20: If you were to ask your boss for a raise, what would be your reasoning?

Anyone who approaches their boss for a raise is under internal pressure from a real or perceived lack of recognition and appreciation. Loyalty is a function of appreciation. Interviewers might ask this question in an attempt to measure your emotional maturity or to see whether you're capable of making a reasoned argument from fact. If you go emotional or personal, you've bombed.

WORST ANSWER: I deserve it. I need it. My personal situation demands more money. I can't afford my [house, car, vacation, in-laws, insurance, private school].

BEST ANSWER: Solid contributions that positively affect the company's bottom line. If you answer this question from the company's point of view, you'll stand out as a team player who has the firm's best interests at heart.

> *Example: "I would point out how I cut expenses in my department 14 percent by renegotiating a shipping contract, not replacing a gentleman who retired, canceling two fax lines that we rarely used, and eliminating the customary practice of overtime for the secretarial pool. Further, I reassigned territories for 3 outside salespeople so their travel expenses were reduced. As a result of that particular reassignment, sales actually increased last quarter by 11 percent because those sales people were able to spend more time in front of clients rather than driving."*

Dump the emotion. Rely on facts and figures. Everyone "needs" more money and almost everyone considers themselves underpaid. Using those arguments are weak.

Question 21: Are you willing to relocate or travel?

Regardless of your answer, it would be best to brush this question aside. You would much rather get the best offer you can, then, if traveling or relocation is a big part of the position, decide whether it's worth it. I've spoken with many people who swore they would never travel or relocate only to be offered a position that made their objections seem trivial.

WORST ANSWER: A flat "no" will slam the door shut on this opportunity. But if not traveling or relocating is actually just a preference, do you really want to lose the job offer over it?

BEST ANSWER: First find out where you may have to relocate and how much travel may be involved, then respond. If there truly is no problem, say so enthusiastically. If you do have a reservation, there are two schools of thought on how to handle it.

> 1. Keep your options open. Respond with "no problem" and use the strategy of getting the offer and later make a judgment call whether it's worth it to you personally to relocate or travel. Hopefully, by the time this offer comes through, you may have other offers and can make a better, more informed decision. Why close the door on this opportunity before it has chance to really open? Of course, if you're a little more desperate in three months, you might wish you had not slammed the door on relocating or traveling.
> 2. The second way to handle this question is to voice a reservation, but assert that you'd be open to relocating (or traveling) for the right opportunity.

The answering strategy you choose depends on how eager you are for the job. If you want to take no chances, choose the first approach. If you want to play a little harder-to-get in hopes of generating a more enticing offer, choose the second.

Question 22: What methods have you found to be successful in setting and achieving job objectives for your subordinates?

Many jobs, especially in management, are just a continuous coaching and nurturing process. These positions require far more than just handing an employee a job description. a how-to manual, and a set of expectations then sitting back and drumming your fingers on the desk while the work gets done and you get the praise. Your interviewer is looking for someone who can combine both a formal approach to setting goals and objectives as well as a sensitivity to understanding the need for informal coaching. If you have done the research I've recommended throughout this book, you know what the cultural style of the company is and what is expected.

WORST ANSWER: Anything that puts you at an extreme. No Winnie the Pooh and no Attila the Hun. Look for a balanced approach between the two.

BEST ANSWER: Balance is the key to this answer, if that is the company norm. If this is a place that's run like a drill sergeant's barracks, you should tailor your answer to fit (do you really want to work here?). Otherwise the interviewer could view you as a softy. On the other hand, if this is a very loose and open organization, coming on too strong will also put you in an unfavorable light. See why research is your best friend?

> *Example: "In the supervisory positions I've held, I've always tried to balance the needs of the company with the performance abilities of my employees. It all begins with hiring the right people, of course, people with the ability, willingness, and savvy to get the job done correctly and produce the desired results. Some people respond well to strict and rigid guidelines while others need more coaching and prodding. I try to be adaptable because the company will benefit if I can uncover how to get the best work out of my people."*

Question 23: No question at all.

If you're uncomfortable with silence, you could blow it with the silent treatment. Essentially, the interviewer just sits there, stone faced, silent, and unmoved by the ticking of the clock while you begin to wonder if he believes your last answer. Most interviewers don't use this question ... they're just as uncomfortable as you! If it IS used, it's designed to see how you respond under stress. When you get this silent treatment after answering a particularly difficult question, such as "tell me about your weaknesses", it's intimidating effect can unnerve even the most polished job hunter. Here's how it works:

- You answer a question and then, instead of asking another, the interviewer stares at you in silence.

• You wait, growing a bit uneasy, and there he sits, stone-faced, silent as a ninja, as if to call you a liar.

• You backtrack in your mind what you just said to see if it was potentially untrue. If it was, you start back-pedaling and qualifying your answer. If it WAS 100% true you wonder if you've unknowingly broken some cardinal rule of interviewing etiquette.

• You begin to continue talking, saying more than you have to, while the professional interviewer gives you just enough rope to hang yourself.

WORST ANSWER: Rushing to fill the void of silence, hedging or qualifying your previous answer, or shifting around in your chair, looking rather uncomfortable. Don't ramble and don't think you just goofed up.

BEST ANSWER: The Silent Treatment loses all its power to frighten you once you refuse to be intimidated and you realize that the interviewer is just as uncomfortable. If your interviewer pulls it, keep quiet yourself for a few seconds and then ask, with sincere politeness and not even a hint of sarcasm, "Is there anything else I can fill in on that point?" or "Did you have another question about that subject?" That's all there is to it. Remember that he may be laughing on the inside, thinking you were uncomfortable.

Whatever you do, don't let the Silent Treatment intimidate you into talking because you could easily talk yourself out of the position.

Question 24: Would you ever lie for your company?

This question pits two values against each other; in this case loyalty against integrity and the interviewer is keenly aware of your tone, vocal inflection, body language, and whether your pupils dilate. Interviewers are always on the lookout for a loose cannon that could end up backfiring on the company.

WORST ANSWER: I'd do whatever it took to advance my company's agenda. It sounds appealing, but that's the sort of thing that Enron CFO's also told the CEO of the company, Kenneth Lay.

BEST ANSWER: Avoid choosing between two values, giving a positive statement which covers all bases instead.

For some interviewers, that won't cut it and they will press you for an answer. If that happens and you're forced to make a choice, always choose personal integrity. It is the most prized of all values. An employee with a high degree of integrity and a mediocre skill set can hurt the company much less than a highly skilled employee with a low personal integrity level. Interviewers know it and they will almost always pass on someone who demonstrates that characteristic.

Question 25: Tell me about your current company's (profits, marketing plans, development projects, research methods, or other confidential matters).

This is another one of those unfair questions, but you can turn it into an advantage with some diplomacy and tact. If an interviewer asks you to reveal confidential information about any of your employers (past or present), you can feel like you're in a no-win situation. Spill the beans and you could be judged untrustworthy. Clam up and you appear uncooperative, semi-accusatory, or overly suspicious.   This question pits basically your desire to be cooperative against your integrity and when you're faced with any such choice, **always choose personal integrity.** It is a far more valuable commodity than whatever information the company may pry from you because once you hand over the information, your value to this company goes way down.

WORST ANSWER: Falling for this trap and unloading the truck or airing your dirty laundry, even just a little. Some interviewees mistakenly believe that revealing something small will work in their favor but nothing could be farther from the truth. Revealing anything makes you look like a Benedict Arnold.

BEST ANSWER: Never reveal anything confidential about a present or former employer but explain your reluctance diplomatically.

Realize that many companies use interviews to spy on, err I mean, research the competition. It's a perfect win in their eyes. Here in their own office, is an insider from the enemy camp who can reveal much sought after information on the competition's plans, research, financial condition, upcoming projects, contracts they're working on, etc. – and all it costs was an ad on the Internet or newspaper and a little time! On the other hand (and you hope this is the case), the company may be testing your integrity to see if you can be bullied into revealing confidential data.

> *Example, "I certainly want to be as open as I can about that. But I also wish to respect the rights of those who have trusted me with their most sensitive information, just as you would hope to be able to trust any of your key people when talking with a competitor."*

And certainly you can allude to your finest achievements in specific ways that don't reveal the combination to the company safe. But be guided by the golden rule. If you were the owner of your present company, would you feel it ethically wrong for the information to be given to your competitors? If so, steadfastly refuse to reveal it.

I have heard of interviewers and even company presidents who will press a candidate unmercifully for confidential information. If the candidate doesn't reveal anything, either the interviewer or president acts visibly annoyed, peppering the candidate with a barrage of questions. It's all an act.
He   couldn't care less about the information, but this is his way of testing the candidate's character. Only those who stand firm get the job offer.

Question 26: Don't you think you're overqualified for this position?

If you've done your homework and have repeatedly tied your abilities, skills, education, and experience to the interviewer's needs, this question shouldn't come up, but if it does, there are two potential reasons. The first is the interviewer seriously DOESN'T think you're the right person for the job. Using this question is a nice way of saying, "No thanks but good luck." The second stems from a   concern you'll grow dissatisfied and leave soon after getting started. This presents a potentially embarrassing situation for an interviewer.

WORST ANSWER: An unprepared answer that stammers, stutters, or otherwise sounds (and looks) confused.

BEST ANSWER: This question is an open invitation to teach the interviewer a new way to think about this situation, seeing advantages instead of drawbacks.

> *Example: "Well, 'overqualified' can be a relative term, depending on how tight the job market is. And right now, it's very tight. I understand and accept that. I also believe that there could be very positive benefits for both of us in this match. Because of my unusually strong experience in [X] , I could start to contribute right away, perhaps much faster than someone who'd have to be brought along more slowly. There's also the value of all the training and years of experience that other companies have invested tens of thousands of dollars to give me. You'd be getting all the value of that without having to pay an extra dime for it. With someone who has yet to acquire that experience, he'd have to gain it on your dime. When it comes to knowing how to work well with people and getting the most out of them, there's just no substitute for what you learn over many years of front-line experience. You company would gain all this, too."*

NOTE: The main concern behind the "overqualified" question is that you will leave your new employer as soon as something better comes your way. Anything you can say to demonstrate the sincerity of your commitment to the employer and reassure him that you're looking to stay for the long-term will help you overcome this objection.

Question 27: Tell me about your persistence (analytical skills, creative problem solving, management ability, etc.).

This is a behavioral type question that can only be answered if you've prepared your stories as recommended. If you have, this question is an easy one to answer!

WORST ANSWER: The cardinal sin here is simply being unprepared. Hesitation makes it seem that you're having a difficult time recalling the last time you were persistent, analytical, creative, or managerial.

BEST ANSWER: Remember Question 2? If you've committed to memory a list of your greatest and most recent achievements, it's easy to present any of your achievements in context of the particular quality the interviewer is quizzing you about.

> *Example: "Last quarter, I was asked to attempt to revive the Perkins account. Mrs. Perkins had been a long time customer but for the past two years, she had consistently moved her business to our greatest competitor and no one knew why. I was determined to find out, so I asked her to meet with me. She said no. I asked again the next week. She still said no. I asked her to meet me for coffee. She again said no. These weekly calls went on for two months. Then I stopped calling for a few weeks and sent her some literature about our newest product line, following up a day later just to make sure she received it. On the call, she asked if I was going to try to set up a meeting with her again. I told her no, that I just wanted to keep her informed on what the latest product was in our industry. I sent her a DVD about our new product and followed up a week later. She asked again if I was going to try to set up a meeting. Again I told her no. Later that week she called my boss (whom I was keeping informed about this whole process) and demanded to know why no one would meet with her. He told her he would "make" me call her and when I did, two days later, she committed to a modest purchase. Over the last 6 months, we've been able to get back 120% of what we lost. Persistence? Its a tool in my toolbox that I know how to use and I use it often."*

Question 28: Tell me how you deal with angry or frustrated customers (employees, suppliers, etc.)

Interviewers want to insure that you have a cool head and that you don't fly off the handle when things don't exactly go your way. Levelheaded employees don't get the company in hot water like their choleric counterparts might. If you're interviewing for a position that regularly meets with the public, deals with employees in a supervisory position, or handles a vendor relationship, I strongly advise you to be prepared for this question.

WORST ANSWER: Saying, "Well, the customer is always right!" allowing the passion of the situation to force you into making a decision one way or another. Or suddenly appearing defensive because you specifically remembered being taken advantage of.

BEST ANSWER: A levelheaded, reasoned response. Interviewers want to see your decision making processes and how you arrive at whatever decision you're faced with.

> *Example: "When dealing with someone who's angry or frustrated, I've found that people want to be heard first and foremost. So, I listen. After their initial volley, I like to ask, "What would you like me to do?" Sometimes they just want to vent and I let them. Sometimes I have to take things a step farther. If I do, I want them to feel a small sense of power, so I ask their permission to take some notes and ask a few questions. At this point, I'm able to gather some pertinent information and find out the key players involved. I tell the person that I'd like to gather a little more information and that I will be back in touch with them by a certain time or date – and I STICK TO IT! Then, because every situation has at least two sides, I get in touch with those key players and gather more facts and opinions. At that point I'm better able to communicate with the angry or frustrated person and tell them which course of action we're going to take to help alleviate their frustrations."*

Question 29: Have you had much experience in firing employees?

The real question in the interviewer's mind isn't just if you can handle the emotional trauma that inevitably rises up within you when firing an employee, but also if you have the judgment to do so. The interview may also be trying to uncover whether you have a soul or if you're just a tyrant. If you've been responsible for hiring in your department, firing a lot of people could reflect poorly on your judgment as well.

WORST ANSWER: Boasting about how many people you've fired, or acting in any way that you enjoyed it.

BEST ANSWER: Describe the rational and sensible management processes you follow when firing an employee. It should always be a last resort (unless there is a large reduction in force). The best reasons to fire someone include insubordination, failure to meet defined objectives, willful violation of policy, violence, etc. If you can turn this question into a positive, you'll be much better off. Move the discussion to what steps you take to insure you don't have to fire someone.

Example: "My whole approach is to do it right on the front end by hiring right. I try to hire the best people, train them well, make sure they're excited and proud to be part of our team, and then work with them to achieve our goals together. If you do all of that, especially hiring the right people, I've found you don't have to fire very often. So with me, firing is a last resort. Do I like it? No, of course not, but when it's got to be done, it's got to be done, and the faster and cleaner, the better. A poor employee can wreak terrible damage in undermining the morale of an entire team of good people. When there's no other way, I've found it's better for all concerned to act decisively in getting rid of offenders who won't change their ways."

Question 30: Tell me about a time something you did – *or didn't do that you should have* – that you now feel embarrassed about.

Some questions should be off limits and this one certainly qualifies, but answering, "none of your business," probably isn't the best idea. Some interviewers ask this question wondering if you'll admit to something, but even if you don't/can't/won't, at least they'll see how you think on your feet. Unprepared candidates (not you!), flustered by this question, tend to unburden themselves of guilt from their personal life or career, perhaps voicing regrets about a parent, spouse, child, college class, etc. All such answers can be disastrous to your job hunting prospects.

WORST ANSWER: Anything of any significance.

BEST ANSWER: Never confess a regret, but never come across as a stone-waller either. Tell the interviewer you have no regrets, then add a habit you practice regularly for healthy human relations.

Example: (strategic pause) "You know ... I really can't think of anything." (pause again) "I would say that as a general management principle, the best way to avoid regrets is to avoid causing them. That can only happen if you're really paying attention to your people and your processes. I like to mentally review each day's events and conversations to take a second look at the projects and people I'm working with and do a double-check of what they're likely to be feeling. Sometimes I'll see things that do need more follow-up, whether a pat on the back, or maybe a five minute chat in someone's office to make sure they're on track with the team. I let each team member know I expect excellence in their performance and I work to set an example myself and I let them all know that I appreciate and respect their feelings. The result is a highly motivated team that's having fun at work because they're striving for excellence rather than brooding over slights or regrets."

Question 31: Tell me about the strengths and weaknesses of your boss (company, executive management team, etc).

Dirty laundry always stinks.   Skillful interviewers can make it almost irresistible to air a little dirty laundry from your previous position.   **DON'T**. There is nothing wrong with some praise for your previous company, however.

WORST ANSWER: Anything negative. Never give in to the temptation no matter how subtly you're persuaded to be critical.

BEST ANSWER: Stress only generic good points. You could mention that your previous boss was easy to talk with, that she was on top of her game, or that the company had a strong commitment to R&D. Just make sure these points never contradict something you've already said or that they cause the interviewer to be concerned that HIS firm doesn't measure up. (Review Question 4)

You may not realize it, but chances are very good that your interviewer doesn't give a rip about your previous boss, company, or management team. He wants to find out how loyal and positive you are, and whether you'll criticize him behind his back if pressed to do so by someone in this company. Remember that today's HR managers view behavioral interviewing as the best way to interview and "the most accurate predictor of future performance is past performance." Criticize THEM today and you will probably criticize US tomorrow is how they think. This question is your opportunity to demonstrate your loyalty to those you work with and for.

Question 32: Tell me about the most boring job you've ever had.

Sounds like fun right? Tell the interviewer about stuffing envelopes for your uncle's direct mail company and guess what – you become associated with this boring job in the interviewer's mind. Every time he sees an envelope, he will think of how bored *you* were. This isn't the type of mental image you want your interviewer to have.

WORST ANSWER: A memorable description of an incredibly boring job.

BEST ANSWER: You refuse to allow yourself to grow bored on any job you've ever held and you can't understand it when others let themselves fall into that rut.

> *Example: "Maybe I've been fortunate in that I've   never looked at work as boring. I also believe that in every company or department there are always challenges to be overcome and problems to be solved. If you're bored, it could be because you're not committed to tackling those problems right under your nose, and commitment has always been one of my strong points."*

Question 33: How successful have you been in developing personnel?

Companies crave people who are willing to come alongside others and help them, mentor them, and train them. This is a valuable asset if it's in your personal repertoire.

The old axiom goes, "If you really want to know a subject, teach it."   Your interviewer may be interested in how well you're able to train and develop others. If you've actually trained others and they've been promoted, by all means, toot your own horn, but make sure you're being completely truthful. Things of this nature are easily checked and nothing will torpedo your future more quickly than lying or stretching the truth beyond recognition.

WORST ANSWER: "They don't pay me (enough) to train the newbies." Or any answer that lies – "I trained someone who went on to become a Vice-President!" is easily verified.

BEST ANSWER: The truth. If you've developed people into managers, assistant managers, sales people, or other positions, go ahead and mention it and be proud. Working with and developing someone into a promotable employee is certainly something to be proud of and the company will appreciate knowing that you're a potential mentor. Companies crave people who are willing to come alongside others and help them, mentor them, and train them. This is a valuable asset if it's in your personal repertoire.

Question 34:   Are you applying for other jobs?

Be honest but do not spend a lot of time in this area. Keep the focus on this job and what you can do for this organization. Anything else is just a distraction.

WORST ANSWER: Yes, I'm applying at your competitor! That one ranks right up there with No (translation: I'm not really that motivated).

BEST ANSWER: You are a hot commodity and you're being very selective with the employers that you're interviewing with. Don't act like you're too good for the interviewer's company or he may just finish this interview as a courtesy.

I actually ask this question when I conduct an interview. Why? I want to know if the candidate actually IS a hot commodity. Combined with Question 9 (Why have you been out of work so long?), it gives me an indication whether the candidate is seriously looking for work or is just getting out there because his wife (or mother) wants him out of the house.

Another reason is I've been burned in the past by candidates who enthusiastically come to work for me, then quit 3 weeks later when their "dream job" actually made them the offer. I get the joy of understanding what "job insurance" is at that point – I was just the backup plan, the job plan B if you will.

Question 35: What are your other career options at this point?

Closely related to the above question, this one wants to find out just how desperate you really are. Remember – **You Are Not Desperate**!

WORST ANSWER: "I need a job ... badly." No one wants someone who's back is against the wall although in some circles, interviewers believe this makes for a decent employee – kind of a "Where else is he going to go? He can be offered a position at the bottom of our range." mentality.

BEST ANSWER: Position yourself as a desired commodity. If you're working currently, explain your potential career path at your present company and why, though you're greatly appreciated there, you're looking for something more (challenge, opportunities for professional growth, money, responsibility, etc.). Also state that you're seriously exploring career opportunities with one or two other firms. You don't have to mention these firms by name. If asked, simply smile and say that you're not a liberty to disclose that information.

If you're currently unemployed, talk about other employment possibilities you're investigating, but tread lightly and speak only in very general terms. You don't want to seem manipulative or occupationally flirtatious.

Question 36: Have you missed more than two days in a row (other than a scheduled vacation) in any of your previous positions?

Despite the mad rush to work from home or telecommute or come in to the office only a few days each week, most companies require their employees to show up on a regular basis. If you've had an attendance problem, don't lie. These things are too easily verified but if you DO admit to having an attendance problem, you could paint yourself as unreliable.

WORST ANSWER: Lying or telling the truth without any explanation ... unless the answer is no.

BEST ANSWER: No. But if you have had no problem, emphasize your consistent attendance record throughout your entire career. If you *have* had a problem, you'd best have a really good explanation. Your best bet is to minimize it and make it crystal clear that it was an aberrant circumstance who's cause has been corrected.

> *Example: "Yes, in 2009 I contracted the flu virus and missed 4 days of work while I recovered. I made certain to stay in touch with my office, both to update my boss on my recovery and to insure that nothing was being overlooked by my staff. I hated missing that much work, but I also didn't want the entire office to be exposed to the virus because I was too bull-headed to stay home and recuperate. One good thing is that I should be immune now!"*

Also describe how important you believe consistent attendance is for a key employee and that you strive to set the best example for any other employees.

> *Example: "I believe it was Woody Allen who said, 'Eighty percent of success is just showing up,' and I fully believe that to do a great job, the first step is showing up!"*

Question 37: You seem to have changed jobs quite frequently. Why?

If your resume or job application needs extra pages, your interviewer may fear you'll leave this position after a short time. Remember that HR managers believe the most accurate predictor of future performance is past performance. He's concerned you may not know what you want, be unstable, or a "problem" who doesn't play well with others.

WORST ANSWER: Going on the defensive, blaming others, or acting like the interviewer doesn't know what he's talking about.

BEST ANSWER: Before the interview stage, work to minimize your appearance as job hopper. If your job history includes several stints that only lasted a few months, remove the ones that don't have any relevance to this position or industry.

Example: Instead of showing five positions like this:

From July 1998 to Oct 2004 – Position A (relevant)
From Nov 2004 to Dec 2004 – Position B (Christmas job)

From Jan 2005 to Feb 2005 – Position C (irrelevant temporary position)
From Feb 2005 to March 2008 – Position D   (relevant)
From April 2008 to Current – Position E   (relevant)

Try re-working them to show only relevant positions:
From July 1999 to Oct 2004 – Position A   (relevant)
From Feb 2005 to March 2008 – Position D   (relevant)
From April 2008 to Current – Position E   (relevant)

It's looking better already! Notice how removing those two small jobs cleans up your resume and application. If you're asked about the gap, you should mention that, yes, you took a few temporary jobs over the Holidays while you were interviewing and seeking Position D. Don't lie about it, but don't focus on those irrelevant positions either.

If this question comes up during your interview, it's up to you to reassure the interviewer that you're no job hopper. Describe each of your relevant positions as part of an overall pattern of growth and career progression, but always be careful that you **don't blame other people for your frequent changes**. However, you can and should point out if changes were beyond your control.

> *Example: I was aware of an upcoming acquisition of my company and I knew that the other company would want to achieve some economies of scale. They already had a strong sales manager for my product line, so to avoid getting the ax,   I made a strategic career move before your department came under the scrutiny."*

Don't worry if your job changes were more frequent when you were just starting your career and were establishing yourself. Those changes are generally looked upon as you rounding out your skills and looking for the right career path. But be sure and mention to your interviewer that at this stage in your career, you're much more interested in the best long-term opportunity.

Another strong option is to highlight the job(s) where you stayed the longest, describing those situations as what you're looking for now.

Question 38:   What kind of person would you

refuse to work with?

Do not be trivial and don't joke around here. It would take disloyalty to the organization, violence or lawbreaking to get you to object. Minor objections will label you as a whiner.

WORST ANSWER: Something silly, a joke, anything trivial, or lying and saying, "I can work with anyone!"

BEST ANSWER: Look the interviewer in the eye and tell him you believe that you can work with or around, most anyone, but that some activities and attitudes are off limits. These would include violating the company's trust, someone who advocated violence either on the clock or off, someone who breaks the law, or someone who encouraged others to do any of these things.

You should mention specific examples where you have carried more than your weight, stopped co-workers from gossiping or sharing unverified rumors, or pulled someone to the side and politely asked them to help you keep a good attitude with the team. If a team runs on morale, you are willing to carry the torch.

Question 39: Tell me about the most fun you've had on a job.

Don't take this question lightly. It represents an opportunity to highlight your accomplishments. Talk about having fun by accomplishing something for the organization you were working for at the time.

WORST ANSWER: The time you put a rubber snake on the secretary's desk, the time you watched a sporting event when you were supposed to be working, or how you won the office pool on the Super Bowl.

BEST ANSWER: Relate an experience that highlights your personal achievements and that matches what the company needs most. For you, getting things done is fun. Hitting your goals is fun. Making a difference and having an impact is fun. Getting people motivated is fun.

> *Example: "I think the most fun I've ever had was when I organized our company's international trade show booth. We had a small team of five people but we all worked well together and were voted Best In Show by*

the other participants in the show. What I really liked was the camaraderie we all shared. One member wasn't too enthusiastic about working on the project, but I was able to get her on board by showing her how important our international presence was. Once she understood that, she was an active participant."

Question 40:   What position do you prefer on a team working on a project?

You must know what the interviewer is looking for if this question arises. Is the company looking for a solid leader or looking to fill a role that does more following? You might pick up this information from the job description, but recognize that almost every role requires a little bit of leading AND a little bit of following. It is best to answer this question generically, but indicate that you are flexible.

WORST ANSWER: Saying you always have to be the leader.

BEST ANSWER: Let the interviewer know you are comfortable in different roles. Unless you're the sole owner of a business, every employee at every company reports to someone, even the CEO reports to the Board of Directors.

> *Example: "Having been in the workforce for [X] years, I've learned that a truly valuable employee is able to switch back and forth. On one project in particular, I was expected to follow the lead of a very experienced employee who was the project manager. She was fabulous and well respected and we were moving ahead on schedule and under budget. we had some disagreements but my job was to keep her completely informed and to follow her lead. About midway though the project's life, however, she accepted another position with a different company and I was asked to step in as the new project leader. I'm happy and proud to say that we were able to finish that project under budget and one week before the deadline. As a result, we were able to start the sales process one week earlier."*

Question 41: When I check your references, what will previous supervisors say your strongest point

is?

This question is strongly related to "What is your greatest strength?" and your answer depends on what the interviewer is looking for. Don't bother with too many vagaries like loyalty, energy, attitude, leadership, expertise, initiative, patience, hard worker, creativity, problem solver, etc, because anyone can memorize a list of positive qualities. Use a positive quality only as it applies to the company's greatest needs and wants.

The truth? I'd be surprised , given our litigious society and the fear of lawsuits, if ANY supervisor responded with more than hire dates and if you're re-employable.

WORST ANSWER: Vagueness, pie-in-the-sky answers of positive characteristics with no examples.

BEST ANSWER: Any positive characteristic that matches the company's needs and wants provided it is backed up with an example.

> *Example: "I believe my boss would highlight my expertise in the customer service field because of how I handled one customer in particular ... [continue with short, successful story]. At another of my jobs, that boss might point out my energy and enthusiasm. I simply LOVE working in this field and it shows because of ... [another short, successful story]."*

Never lose an opportunity to match your successes, your experiences, your education, your achievements with this company's greatest needs or wants as determined by your research. Aggressively seek those opportunities and your interview may be cut short ... because they want to offer you the job!

Question 42: Give me an example of your initiative in a challenging situation.

Here is another behavioral interviewing question. The interviewer is trying to gage your ability to see what needs to be done and get to it. Make sure you tailor your response to the company or industry. If you're interviewing for a marketing position you probably don't want to answer this question with an answer that highlights your legal prowess. By the same token, if you're interviewing for a position in the purchasing department, pointing out how you researched options for saving money when you worked in an accounts receivable position may affirm to the interviewer that you watch your pennies.

WORST ANSWER: Not being prepared or mentioning something irrelevant to the position. Taking the initiative to balance your checkbook, for example.

BEST ANSWER: Again, matching your initiative story to what the interviewer wants to hear.

> *Example: "Funny you should ask that, I was just thinking the other day about how I had trained a new hire on my own, without any prodding from my boss. I believe that a well trained team functions better, so that would be one example. Another would be on my last job. I had several complicated processes for filling out paperwork so we could be reimbursed quickly. I took the time to document what was important with each of those forms and wrote a manual on the entire process, just so I wouldn't forget any steps. I asked the management information systems department to make it available on our company intranet and it became a standard training practice to use that manual for all new hires in my department."*

Question 43: Tell me about the worst (job related) decision you ever made.

This one is closely related to Question 3, "What is your greatest weakness?" but you need to approach it just as carefully. Some interviewers are keen on getting you to admit a weakness or a flaw and this question is designed to do just that.

WORST ANSWER: Admitting to a mistake that is a key component with this position.

BEST ANSWER: It needs to be something trivial as it relates to **this**   job. It can range from getting too far ahead of the rest of your team on a project to following company policy when your instincts told you otherwise (giving a thieving assistant manger the alarm code, for example). Follow up with what you learned from this mistake and you'll hit a home-run with your interviewer.

Example: "I had been named to work on a very important project for my company and I was thrilled to be on that team. I guess my enthusiasm got the best of me because I worked 16 hour days on it and my portion of the project was completed far ahead of the rest of the team. There were some minor adjustments made by the customer along the way, but because I was so far ahead on my part, I wasn't aware of those changes. It wasn't anything I couldn't correct, but I learned that I need to keep a better pace with the rest of the team and keep the project leader consistently informed about my progress."

Question 44: Tell me about your dream job.

Stay away from anything specific, especially the job you're interviewing for right now. If you tell the interviewer that this job is your "dream job," he won't believe you and your credibility will be stretched thin. If you say another job is it, you'll make the interviewer suspicious that you'll be dissatisfied with this position if he hires you. The best answer is to stay generic and leave the specifics until after you're hired.

WORST ANSWER: This one (too obvious), or a job with Company A as a [position]. Another poor answer is anything that makes you look lazy or that attempts humor.

BEST ANSWER: Go a bit more generic than you think. Answer "a job where I love the work, like the people, can contribute and can't wait to get to work."

Example: "I think my dream job is one where I'm fulfilled and happy with the contribution I can make. Work defines a lot of people and I'm one of those who derives a lot of personal satisfaction from my job. My dream job would be one where I get along well with my co-workers and would be able to grow professionally and personally as a result of being there."

Question 45: Have you ever been asked to leave a position? or Have you ever been fired?

If you have been fired, be honest, be brief, and avoid saying negative things about the people or organization involved.

If you haven't, say no, of course, and move on. If you have, be honest, brief, and avoid saying negative things about the people or organization involved. As I mentioned in Question 4, these things are too easily discovered, so always be honest but deflect this negativity by taking the high road and refusing to go negative.

WORST ANSWER: A lie, or saying yes with a weak explanation.

BEST ANSWER: If you have been fired previously,   try doing something totally unnatural: describe your own firing – candidly, succinctly and without a trace of bitterness – from the company's point-of-view, indicating that you could understand why it happened and you might have made the same decision yourself given similar circumstances. Taking this simple step will demonstrate a high degree of professionalism and class, but it has to be sincere. You will stand head and shoulders above the legions of fired employees who claim victim status and who, at the slightest provocation, plop down on their therapist couch to decry the unfairness of it all.

Example: "I was asked to leave a position several years ago after I had instructed an employee to recover a damaged piece of equipment from outside. Someone had been misusing a forklift and it was stuck in a ditch. The weather was supposed to turn extremely cold and the internal workings of that piece of machinery would have been damaged, perhaps beyond repair. The proper thing to do was to inform my regional safety manager what was going on, but since it was late, I made a quick decision to save the company $30,000 and get that machinery pulled inside the building. The company felt I was being insubordinate by making this decision without consulting corporate and I was asked to leave. I can understand the company's position and I harbor no bitterness but if given the same chance again, I would still put the company's best interests first."

Question 46: If you were hiring someone for this job, what would YOU look for?

Here is your chance to shine. Since you've already uncovered the details about this position, what the interviewer and company wants accomplished by this position, and you've lined up your achievements with what the company needs, you're in a perfect position to describe yourself without coming across as a braggart.

WORST ANSWER: Describing someone other than yourself, or saying "ME!" Answering ME is just to obvious. You need to be a little more coy.

BEST ANSWER: Be careful to mention traits that are needed and that you have. Use the interviewer's lingo and the exact wording of the job description if possible.

> *Example: "As I understand it, this position needs someone who has plenty of experience in the field, so I would specifically look for that. I would also look for people who know how to organize a team and lead it whether as the team leader or as a member. I would also make certain that the candidate had the proper drive to get the job done and I would look for specific instances in his or her past experience to certify his or her claims."*

Question 47: What do you look for when you hire people?

This may not be a function of the position your interviewing for presently, but many companies want to know that you have some management savvy and that you can read people, even if on just a very basic level.

WORST ANSWER: Being unprepared for the question or describing someone just like yourself.

BEST ANSWER: Feel free to speak your own ideas here, but for the best answer weave them around the four most important qualifications for any position.

1. Do they have the qualifications? (can they do the work?)

2. Do they have the motivation? (will they do it?)
3. Is this person our kind of team player? (will they fit our culture?)
4. Do they have character? (do they possess integrity)?

You can have the first three, but if number four is lacking you'll eventually have a problem. I've seen it happen too many times.

Question 48:   Are you a team player?

Of course you're a team player! Don't be afraid to say so, but be sure to have examples and stories ready to back up your claim. Good evidence of your team attitude will include   specifics showing that you often perform for the good of the team rather than for yourself. Don't brag, just say it in a matter-of-fact tone. Don't talk about how you worked in a team of 6, but only 2 of you did the work and don't talk about how you "held a team together." The interviewer isn't looking for glue, he's looking for common goals, shared experiences, how you worked together and shared the jobs amongst the team members. He wants to know about the general harmony of the entire group and above all, he wants to know if you're capable of being part of a successful team – as evidenced by your past experiences.

WORST ANSWER: A simple yes without specific examples to back it up. Let's face it, no one is probably ever going to answer this question with a no.

BEST ANSWER: Using specifics, lay out the foundation that you're a team player and then build upon it with examples.

If you're asked this teamwork question, be sure and talk about the team, what you did well, how you all overcame obstacles, your specific role, what you learned, did you meet the deadline, were you under or over budget and why. Above all talk about the team's success.

Question 49: Looking back on your career, do you think you've you done your best work?

Trick question alert!   Answer "absolutely" and it seems as if your best work is behind you. Answer, "no, my best work is ahead of me," and it seems as if you didn't give 100 percent on your other jobs. Such is the quandary of a job candidate! But the interviewer is probably laughing inside. This question is a false dichotomy – that is, it makes you choose between one or the other, but there is more than just one possible answer.

WORST ANSWER: Yes or no.

BEST ANSWER: To cover all the angles, answer neither! Tell the interviewer that you always try to do your best, and the best of your career is **right now**, in the present. Like an athlete at the top of his game, you are just hitting your career stride thanks to your outstanding qualifications. You guessed it – those qualifications mysteriously align with what the interviewer wants or needs most out of a candidate for this open position.

Question 50: Explain how you would be an asset to this organization.

Finally! You should be anxious for this question. It's the one you've been waiting for all day. It gives you a chance to highlight your best points as they relate to the position being discussed.

WORST ANSWER: Any answer that doesn't align your achievements and abilities with the organization's needs and wants.

BEST ANSWER: Take a moment and "act" like you're thinking about the answer. Then slowly begin telling the interviewer what you understand are the company's needs and how your experience, achievements, education, and abilities strangely match exactly those needs. It appears that you are a perfect fit for what the interviewer is looking for.

> *Example: "You know, just playing over in my mind what we've discussed so far today, I believe you're looking for someone with extensive web design experience in MySql, PHP, and CSS and it's really odd how my professional experience with each of those matches. So first of all, I am perfectly qualified to help you meet your goals and objectives when it comes to web design. Not only that, but I'm enrolled in some classes at night that will further my abilities in each of those areas. But going beyond just the qualifications you have on paper, I'm also well versed in leading teams, communicating between departments with different agendas, and setting and achieving goals, both personal and professional. You've mentioned the importance of all those*

attributes today and I'm stunned quite frankly at how well I match up."

Question 51: What qualities do you look for in a boss?

Stay on the safe side and give a generic yet positive type of answer. Bosses love to think highly of themselves (don't we all) so if you're being interviewed by your potential boss, answering with a broad and generic answer will keep you safe. Avoid mentioning anything from a negative viewpoint because it will make it seem as though you're complaining about a previous boss in a subtle way

WORST ANSWER: Someone who is NOT [a jerk, always late for meetings, a micro-manager, etc].

BEST ANSWER: Safe qualities are knowledgeable, a sense of humor, fair, loyal to subordinates and holder of high standards. All bosses think they have these traits.

> *Example: "I very much enjoy working with someone who has the knowledge and capabilities to do their job very well, who emulates the high standards of a person in a position in authority, who holds everyone accountable for their work, and who is fair and loyal to his or her employees. A sense of humor is a plus!"*

Question 52: Tell me about a time when you helped resolve a dispute between others.

Pick a specific incident from your experience – it doesn't have to be anything major, but you do need to have the story at the forefront of your mind. Once you start relating what happened, the dispute itself isn't what's important. What IS important is the problem solving technique you used and why you used it.

WORST ANSWER: Highlighting the "he said/she said" aspects of any dispute or going into far too much detail. It's almost as bad as not having an answer prepared at all.

BEST ANSWER: Give the extremely short version of the event, then focus on the problem solving techniques you used to bring resolution to the dispute. Did you launch an investigation? How did you word the questions you asked of the people involved? Did you suspect you were being used? How did you handle any emotional outbursts? What were the results of your handling the dispute?

Question 53. How would you respond to your boss if he was in love with an idea that you thought was horrible?

Here we are with another question that positions two values against each other, in this case loyalty to your boss (and by default to your company) and honesty.

WORST ANSWER: Brown-nosing or blurting out something like, "I'd tell him it was crazy!"

BEST ANSWER: Remember the #1 rule of handling conflicts: when choosing between values, always choose integrity. The company doesn't want "yes" men or "yes women" (you hope), but at the same time you have to tactfully explain your point of view to your boss.

> *Example: "Even if I wasn't crazy about his or her idea, there's probably a good chance that there is *something* about it I would like, so I'd begin my approach to my boss with an emphasis on what I liked. Next I would point out areas where I had concerns and the reasoning behind those concerns, being as objective and factual as possible. I owe my boss and my company my honesty because the company is counting on me for that much at a minimum. I would express my thoughts in a constructive way because my goal is to make the company as successful as possible. If I can make my boss' idea stronger, or more appealing, he and I would both win. But if he overrules me and says, 'let's move forward with my idea as is,' then I will throw my full and enthusiastic support behind him and work to make his plans as successful as possible."*

You can't get much better than that. Any boss would love to have an employee with this attitude.

Question 54: What have you done to improve your knowledge in the last year?

Your interviewer wants to know that you're constantly trying to improve yourself. When answering this question, only include improvement activities that relate to your job. A wide variety of activities can be mentioned as positive self-improvement but are not job related. Using one of these isn't going to improve your chances of landing a job offer so have some employment related exercises on hand.

WORST ANSWER: Anything unrelated to the job you're interviewing for. "I learned how to design a website – when you're interviewing for a position managing line workers in a factory."

BEST ANSWER: Carefully tying your self improvement activities to the open position. If you're interviewing for a plant manager position, show how you attended a seminar related to decreasing downtime or how to cut overtime. If you're interviewing for a position in a creative field, mention how you collaborated with a recognize professional or took additional classes to hone your skills. If you haven't taken any such classes or attended any seminars, mention how you've read a book by an expert in the field or conducted research on something that was troubling you.

Important: after you mention one of these activities, make certain you tie what you learned together with an important aspect of the position. Never lose an opportunity to point out how YOU are the best match for what the company needs.

Question 55:   What outside interests do you cultivate?

You want to be well-rounded, not a robot or an idle laggard. But your potential employer would be even more turned off if he suspects that your heavy extracurricular load will interfere with your commitment to your work duties.

WORST ANSWER: None or far too many. Either of these extremes is not going to bode well for your job opportunities.

BEST ANSWER: If you've done some research on this company's culture, you should have some measure of knowledge about how management would view your participation in extracurricular activities. Does the management team participate in triathlons or golf tournaments? Does the company sponsor charity events or are they active members of the Rotary Club or Chamber of Commerce? Those are the kinds of questions you need to have answered before you step foot into the office for an interview.

Feel free to answer this question in a way that shatters any potential stereotypes that could limit your chances of getting a job offer. If you're over 50, for example, describe your activities in ways that demonstrate physical stamina, such as running, walking, bicycling, hiking or any other type of physical exercise. Conversely, if you're young, describe more activities that lead the interviewer to see you as a person of wisdom and someone who invests in the community. You might talk about serving on a local charity, working with Big Brothers Big Sisters and mentoring youth.

But above all, remember that the interviewer is looking for someone who can contribute at work, not just in the community or just for personal interests. No matter how admirable an   activities may be, make sure your answer about it advances your chances for the job offer.

Question 56: Give me an example of a time when you were told "no."

By asking this question your interviewer is trying to gage your emotional maturity level by asking how you handled rejection in the past. Emotionally immature people want instant gratification for their desires, immediate acceptance for their ideas, and quick recognition of their talent or skills. As a group, these people are notorious for their inability to handle rejection, even if that rejection is temporary. *How you answer this question will determine your maturity level in your interviewer's mind.*

WORST ANSWER: Denial that you've ever been told no, not having a story to relate about the experience, or getting defensive.

BEST ANSWER: Laugh ... out loud. Then tell your interviewer that some of the best feedback you've ever gotten was negative feedback. You've learned more from your failures than you ever thought possible. Then quickly turn the conversation into the ways you learned valuable lessons about your job – as they relate to this position.

> *Example: "Ha-ha! Funny you should ask! I was thinking about my career on the way over here this morning and realized how much I've actually learned from rejection than I ever learned from acceptance. When I was selling stocks and other securities right out of college, I was rejected over and over again, mostly because of my youth and inexperience I believe. And I can understand why – who wants to trust their life savings to a rookie? I decided to approach potential clients in a whole new way and use my youth to my advantage. I told them I was young, but I was eager, and that my eagerness to earn their trust would cause me to work harder for them than any other stockbroker they've seen. I reminded clients that I was from the information generation and that I could easily and quickly find them the information they required to make great investment decisions. As a result, my sales began to climb and the trust those people had in me grew as well."*

Question 57: What do you do when a decision needs to be made, but no procedure exists?

The interviewer is keenly interested in how you'll approach an unconventional situation. In the back of his mind, he's wondering if you'll stick to the rules or if you'll devise some new system based on the whims of the moment. Always indicate that you'll seek counsel and guidance when you're faced with something of this nature.

WORST ANSWER: I "wing it" or anything that indicates you'll fail to get some guidance.

BEST ANSWER: Approach the boss, or if she isn't available, go further up the chain of command. If no one is available, indicate that you would seek guidance from someone on the same level as your boss. At all times, stick to the rules.

> *Example: "Actually, that's happened to me before. What I did was first approach my boss with as much information as was available and asked for her input. She really appreciated my not shooting from the hip since there wasn't a procedure in place. Had she not been available, I would have sought the advice from her boss or from one of*

her peers. If that wasn't an option, or if there wasn't anyone available for whatever reason, I would make certain I followed company guidelines as closely as possible and take careful notes of what I did, why, who was involved, and what was communicated so that when I was eventually able to contact her, I would have all my information readily available."

Question 58: The "chink in your armor" question.

If an interviewer has read your resume carefully, he may try to zero in on a "fatal flaw" he sees with your work history, your education (or lack thereof) or some other aspect of your background. Maybe you don't have an advanced degree or you've been out of the job market for quite a while, or your certification has expired. These questions are really just concerns about your future performance and you should be able to alleviate those concerns based on your past performance in similar situations.

WORST ANSWER: Getting defensive or downplaying the interviewer's concerns without specific examples showing why he needn't be worried.

BEST ANSWER: Without spending too much time acknowledging your "fatal flaw," tell the interviewer the ways you plan to overcome it. Tell him about ways you've overcome it in the past and be specific. Use numbers or statistics to back up your ability to perform well. If it relates to being out of the job market, tell the interviewer the ways you've kept up with trends in the industry, trade journals you read, networking contacts you maintain.

Question 59: Tell me about the last book you read.

Never attempt to fake it, no matter what. No one expects you to be a bookworm, but it never hurts to indicate that you're interested in keeping up with recent books in your profession. If nothing else, read reviews of books on the Internet. Bloggers review books all the time, so benefit from their synopsis of the most recent or influential book in your industry.

WORST ANSWER: Faking it and acting like you know what you're talking about. Blank stares are pretty bad too.

BEST ANSWER: Reading is almost always done on personal time and demonstrates a commitment to learning outside the workplace. If you're already committed to reading on a regular basis, this question is a no brainer, but if you haven't read anything since *Huck Finn* in the eleventh grade, invest the time to find out what books are considered important in your industry. How do you find this out? Ask people IN the industry. Then either buy the book, read it and take notes, or perform a Google search on the book followed by the word "review" and see what sites have already read it. Many of these sites will give you a synopsis that can help you NOT look like a dullard.

Question 60: Tell me about a time you felt adequately recognized for a job well done.

This is another emotional maturity question. Tell the interviewer that you don't expect a pat on the back every time you do your job, after all, it IS your job and you're supposed to do it well. But at the same time, you do like to be recognized (like 99 percent of the rest of the world, your interviewer included).

WORST ANSWER: Anything that indicates a lack of emotional maturity, pettiness, or trends toward the negative.

BEST ANSWER: Recognition and encouragement by management is what makes you feel great about working with someone.

> *Example: "I believe everyone needs recognition and encouragement from time to time, but it should be something that's handed out only when it's truly deserved, otherwise it becomes diluted and worthless. I personally feel adequately recognized when my boss gives me credit for my ideas, and takes a moment every so often to make certain I'm on track. The best recognition is solid feedback."*

Question 61: In what ways has your current boss contributed to your decision to search for another job?

Trick question alert! The interviewer is trying to get you to step off into a negative mud pit and wallow around. <u>Refuse to do it.</u> Never under any circumstances go negative. Tell your interviewer that you have nothing negative to say about your current boss or company and that the reasons you're looking for another position is to grow professionally, to make more income, to learn more about the industry, to contribute more, to advance your career, etc.

WORST ANSWER: My boss was a jerk and [blah, blah, blah]. You might as well get up and walk out of the interview. It's THAT damaging.

BEST ANSWER: Studies confirm that 80 percent of all job resignations originate with the quitting employee's boss. People don't quit a job, they quit a boss! Your interviewer knows this little statistic and, since the numbers would indicate that you quit your boss, he wants to know if you'll turn on him or her. Your best answer is to be positive about your current (or former) situation and say only the best things possible. It's hard sometimes, but finding something positive to say is an exercise that strengthens your candidacy.

> *Example: "Oh, my boss hasn't contributed to my decision. I only have positive things to say about her. The reason I'm in the job market is to ... [advance my career, grow professionally, earn a higher salary, etc]. I believe your company can help me do that and I believe that with my experience in this industry, I can help you [meet your greatest need]. My history proves it, my education backs it up, and my record of achievements shows that I'm a perfect fit."*

Question 62: Can you recall a time when you or your team missed a deadline because no one realized it was a priority?

Almost everyone has missed a deadline at some point in their lives, but you should never reveal that you missed an *important* deadline. The interviewer is asking this question to measure:

> 1. Your resistance to stressful situations. The more stress resistant an employee is, the greater the likelihood he or she will miss a deadline.
> 2. If your relaxed nature rubs off on others, causing them to lack a sense of urgency.

WORST ANSWER: Revealing that you missed a deadline that cost the company a significant amount of money or one from which you couldn't recover. Claims of perfection in this area are pretty weak as well – you might be embarrassed when the interviewer checks your references.

BEST ANSWER: Recount a situation where there were stages of deadlines and you missed the first one, but recovered in time to meet the others. Be careful that you don't blame someone else for missing it, no matter if it was their fault. Always take responsibility.

> *Example: "I was responsible for training a new assistant manager through a series of 8 study courses and she was to be tested at the end of each of 8 weeks. Our work week started on Mondays but she started working on a Tuesday. I incorrectly thought she would start the testing after working one full week but discovered that her first test was late because of my assumption. She was exceptionally bright and was*

Question 63: Tell me about a time you used your enthusiasm to your advantage.

Remember that enthusiasm was rated by 85 percent of hiring managers as a highly desirable trait. To that end, make certain you have an enthusiasm story at the forefront of your mind so when you're asked this question (or a derivative of it), you can easily move into how your enthusiasm perfectly matches this employer's needs and wants. Why enthusiasm? Enthusiasm stems from a positive attitude whether it's a positive attitude about life, your company, its products, or how those products and services can benefit customers. What would be your personal enthusiasm level if you were responsible for selling a device that could instantly heal a broken bone, or cure depression, or repair a dented car, or communicate with people in a coma? You don't have to cure cancer to be enthusiastic, you only have to believe in what you're doing, and employers LOVE it.

WORST ANSWER: A blank stare or a made up story.

BEST ANSWER: Relate a story from a time when you were new and excited about your job. Remember why you were excited? It probably wasn't because of the money, it was probably because you enjoyed what you were doing. Think back to how that affected your personal work performance and tell THAT story.

> *Example: "I went to work for a window manufacturer a few years back and I was responsible for all our national home show booths. The more I studied the products we were manufacturing, the more I became convinced that they were the best products on the market. I couldn't help but be enthusiastic about how they could help our customers. But that's how I operate: I learn as much as I can so that I can be both confident AND enthusiastic about whatever I'm doing. People love to listed to someone who believes in their products or services and I try my hardest to be that person."*

Question 64: Are you available to work nights and/or weekends?

Ideally, you've already done enough research so that this question doesn't blindside you. Still, there could always be another position the interviewer is thinking of, or there could be some changes coming down the pike that haven't been made public quite yet. Say "no way, not this cowboy" and you can kiss any job offer adiós amigo. But what if you have a family and want to work a reasonably normal schedule? Can you get the job and the schedule you want?.

WORST ANSWER: Lying. It hurts you, your family, and the employer.

BEST ANSWER: Of course, if you consistently burn the midnight oil, this question is a softball lob. Smack it out of the park on the first swing by saying this kind of schedule is just your style. Add that your family understands it. Indeed, they're happy for you, as they know you get your greatest satisfaction from your work.

If however, you prefer a more balanced lifestyle, answer this question by asking: "What are the standard work hours and schedules for your best people here?" You should get a response that will tell you what you want to know. If, however, the hours still sound unrealistic for you, ask, "Do you have any top people who perform exceptionally for you, but who also have families and like to get home in time to see them at night?" Chances are this company does, and this associates you with this other "top-performers-who-leave-not-later-than-six" group.

Above all, be honest. You don't want to have to repeat the job hunting process three months later because you're working 6 nights each week until midnight. Be honest, but phrase your response positively.

Example: "I love my work and do it exceptionally well. I think the results speak for themselves, especially in …(mention your two or three qualifications of greater interest to the employer. Remember, this is what he wants most, not a workaholic with weak credentials). Not only would I bring these qualities, but I've built my whole career on working not just hard, but smart. I think you'll find me one of the most productive people here. I do have a family who likes to see me after work and on weekends. They add balance and richness to my life, which in turn helps me be happy and productive at work. If I could handle some of the extra work at home in the evenings or on weekends, that would be ideal. You'd be getting a person of exceptional productivity who meets your needs with strong credentials. And I'd be able to handle some of the heavy workload at home where I can be under the same roof as my family. Everybody would win."

Question 65: If you had the chance, what would you do differently in your life?

This question is usually asked to uncover any life-influencing mistakes, regrets, disappointments or problems that may continue to affect your personality and performance. Do not want give your interviewer negatives to remember you by, such as some great personal or career disappointment. Even if it was ancient history, dwelling on the past makes you look like a loser. Don't give any answer which could hint that your whole heart and soul will not be in your work.

WORST ANSWER: Whining about the past.

BEST ANSWER: Indicate that you are a happy, fulfilled, optimistic person and that, in general, you wouldn't change a thing.

Example: "[laughing] Hindsight is always 20/20 but since I can't go back and change history, I prefer not to dwell on it. I've had a good life, a lot of learning opportunities and experience, and I feel that the best it yet to come. Every experience in life is a lesson it its own way. I wouldn't change a thing."

Question 66: You've been with your firm a long time. Won't it be difficult to switch to a new company?

Your interviewer may be worried that an old dog (you) will find it hard to learn some new tricks. Your job is to convince him that you can. You accomplish this by demonstrating through your stories and experiences all the different ways you've adapted and overcome.

WORST ANSWER: Yes, maybe, or acting like the interviewer is clairvoyant.

BEST ANSWER: To overcome this objection, outline the many ways you have grown and adapted to changing conditions at your present firm. No one works in a static situation. Highlight the different responsibilities you've held, the wide array of new situations you've faced and conquered. As a result, you've learned to adapt quickly to whatever is thrown at you, and you thrive on the stimulation of new challenges.

To further assure the interviewer, describe the similarities between the new position and your prior one. Explain that you should be quite comfortable working there, since their needs and your skills make a perfect match

Question 67. What do you see as the proper role/mission of:

- a good (job title you're seeking);
- a good manager;
- an employee in the community;
- a leading company in our industry; etc.

"Proper role" questions are designed to examine your understanding of your place in the bigger picture of your department, company, community and profession as well as the proper role each of these entities *should* play. While this question is most frequently asked by only the most thoughtful individuals and companies, it may also pop up by those concerned that you're coming from a place with a radically different corporate culture (such as from a small aggressive company to a big government bureaucracy or a massive corporation).

WORST ANSWER: The most frequent mistake is simply not being prepared (seeming as if you've never given this any thought or phrasing an answer best suited to your prior organization's culture instead of the interviewing company's.

BEST ANSWER: Think of the most essential ingredients of success for each category above – your job title, your role as manager, your firm's role, etc. Identify at least three but no more than six qualities you feel are most important to success in each role. Then commit your response to memory. Here, again, the more information you've already drawn out about the greatest wants and needs of the interviewer, and the more homework you've done to identify the culture of the firm, the more on-target your answer will be.

Question 68: Why should I hire you from the outside when I could promote someone from within?

This question sounds aggressive but it isn't really. It merely represents the interviewer's own dilemma concerning his own worry about hiring someone who could be an unknown commodity. He's probably leaning toward you already but needs some reassurance and wants to hear what you have to say.

WORST ANSWER: Getting flustered because you don't have a good reason.

BEST ANSWER: Help him see the qualifications that only you can offer. If you've done your homework, you already know what he needs and how your qualifications, experiences, education, and achievements match those needs. If this question comes up, you need to either:
- Restate your qualifications and how they match his needs.
- Ask if there are any internal candidates that match your qualifications.

Example: "In general, I think it's a good policy to hire from within – to look outside probably means you're not completely comfortable choosing someone from inside. Naturally, you want this department to be as strong as it possibly can be, so you want the strongest candidate. I feel that I can fill that bill because…(then recap your strongest qualifications that match up with his greatest needs). Are there any internal candidates with these qualifications?

Asking this question is a bold move and you probably won't get a straight answer. But be careful that you don't come off too cocky or aggressive.

Question 69: Give me some examples of how your strengths compliment your boss's management style.

Another trick question. The interviewer is using a subtle question to see if you'll criticize your boss. Many interviewees think they're in the clear with this question because it gives them an opportunity to highlight how they will contribute to the team, but in reality it's a question designed to pinpoint any areas of disagreement between the candidate and management. If you're interviewing for a promotion, it could also be a fishing expedition attempting to uncover areas where your former boss was weak.

WORST ANSWER: Anything that points out where you and your boss disagree. "My organizational skills will help her get on top of things a little better," or "My ability to act as a cushion between him and the other employees will help improve morale" are both criticisms in disguise.

BEST ANSWER: Don't take the bait! Refuse to criticize anyone, even if it's well known or warranted. Always draw attention to YOUR skills as they relate to the job you're interviewing for.

> *Example: "My boss and I get along great and we function well as a team. I think our strengths compliment each other. I have a great deal of respect for her and it's my personal feeling that she respects and values me. As I understand it, this position needs people who can function well together and I'm always looking for ways to improve my job relationships. I think you'll find that I'm [a skillful organizer, a*

*thoughtful leader, a committed team member, or other characteristic
the company wants/needs].*

Question 70: Some people feel that staying at one job for so long demonstrates a lack of initiative. What's your take on that?

This is the question that may be used if your career has been marked by
stability. The interviewer that asks it is measuring your poise and quick
thinking. Yes, it's a sneaky question, but it's a good one for measuring those
characteristics.

WORST ANSWER: Getting flustered or acting like you were blindsided
by the question. Remember, he's looking for poise.

BEST ANSWER: Keep your cool and politely disagree, stating the positive
characteristics that are overlooked by such a position. Give examples of how
you've taken initiative on projects within the company and of the different
hats you've worn. You could turn this one around and ask what the average
tenure is at this company.

> *Example: "Hmm, I've never thought of it that way. I suppose you could
> make that case in a few instances, but it would be rare in my opinion.
> I'd look at the broader picture of loyalty, stability, and commitment
> rather than a lack of initiative. Considering all the different projects
> I've been a part of, my experience may be at one company, but my
> experience has been broadened by [list the projects you were a part
> of]. What I learned from all these experiences is [list what you learned
> in light of what this company wants]."*

If you've been in the exact same job for a very long period of time, that one is
a little tougher. You'll need to emphasize the complexities of what you did,
explaining that the work was challenging and enjoyable.

Question 71: Define [cooperation, management, team-building, marketing, operations, etc]

This "challenge" question is designed to be an open-ended, non-directive type
of question to build a case (one way or the other) concerning your attitude

about the areas mentioned. The interviewer is probably leaning your way already. He wants to see how well your answers will mesh with company culture, traditions, and accepted norms. Since you've done research on this company, your answer will obviously match what he wants to hear.

WORST ANSWER: A stock dictionary definition of any of the terms he mentions. Taking way too long to think about it isn't a good sign either.

BEST ANSWER: If this company is a very collaborative, team-oriented company, obviously your answer would need to reflect those qualities and use words to that effect (collaborate, together, input, support). If it is a highly rigid, top-down type of culture, you'll need to weave in appropriate words like discipline, policy, directives, and chain-of-command.

Question 72: How many projects can you handle at one time?

The interviewer needs to know if you'll run around the office with blinders on until one job is finished or if you can change horses in mid-stream (as is the case in the real world on many days!). If you've uncovered what qualities the interviewer needs in this position, you'll be ahead of the game, able to tailor your response to his needs. Many times this question is followed up with :"How many projects to you *like* to handle at one time?" Both questions are asked for one reason: the position demands someone who can wear many hats at once and multi-task with the best of them. If this is you, don't answer the question with a numerical answer, tell a story instead.

WORST ANSWER: Any number you mention, even if it is a high number. You'll appear ridiculous if you guess high and you'll appear like a dolt if you guess low.

BEST ANSWER: Transition into story-teller mode and relate a story about how you've handled a multitude of things at once. The story should include how you delegated, how you prioritized, and the results of your actions.

Example: "I can handle as many as needed to move the company forward. In a previous position, I was responsible for several projects at once and I think it says something about a person when they're replaced by two people! I love the challenge of work and I've learned some key skills when it comes to handling many different projects. One, you need to know what the highest priority for the company is and two, you have to know how to delegate. Delegation isn't just handing off a job to a subordinate ... no, it's actually knowing each team member's strengths and using those to help drive the project forward, on time and under budget. We were developing a new market and it required a lot of organization and a lot of research ... [continue story]."

You should also consider the possibility that the company is asking because they WANT someone who will work on and finish one thing at a time. In that case, your answer should demonstrate that you have the ability to concentrate and focus until you see a job through to completion.

Question 73: What would you do if a co-worker wasn't pulling his/her weight ...and was hurting your department?

No one wants to hire a hot-head, but no one wants a wimp, either. This question and other hypothetical questions test your sense of human relations and how you might handle office politics. The interviewer is possibly trying to goad you into a complaint session, or could be trying to see how you'll handle the real world fact that no two people are equally productive all the time.

WORST ANSWER: Any answer where you show emotion or anger at past hurts.

BEST ANSWER: Remember what the interviewer is trying to measure – your own ability to handle petty office politics. Office politics are everywhere, in even the most open firms. Any CEO who claims there are no office politics isn't involved enough! To effectively answer this question,   fall back on universal principles of effective human relations – which in the end, are the way you would like to be treated in a similar circumstance.

Example: "Basic good will tells me to go directly to the person and calmly explain the situation, trying to enlist his help in a constructive, positive solution. If I sensed resistance, I would be as persuasive as possible to explain the benefits we all gain from working together, and the problems we, the company and our customers will experience if we don't. One thing I wouldn't do is let the problem slide, because situations like this tend to only get worse and overlooking it would damage morale and set a bad precedent. I would try repeatedly to solve the problem, involving wider and wider circles of people, both above and below the offending co-worker and including my own boss if necessary, so that everyone involved could see the rewards for teamwork and the drawbacks of non-cooperation."

Question 74: What problems do you experience in getting things done?

The interviewer is looking for a chink in your armor and wants you to admit one. Don't. This question asks what you *personally* have found most difficult in previous positions and is a bit difficult to redefine into something positive. Your interviewer will assume that whatever you found toughest may give you a problem in your new position.

WORST ANSWER: Answering the question out-right. "Paperwork" or "customers" or "the union" will all result in your stock losing value right before your eyes.

BEST ANSWER: State that there was nothing in your previous positions that you found overly difficult, and ... stop. Don't say anything else. If pressed to expand upon your answer, describe all the aspects of the position you enjoyed more than others, making sure that you communicate maximum enjoyment for those tasks most important to the open position, and you enjoyed least those tasks that are unimportant to the position at hand.

*Example: "Honestly, I didn't find anything **too** difficult to master, but if I were pressed to answer the question, I'd have to say that I enjoyed the paperwork the least and the interaction with customers the most. I'm most comfortable developing those long term relationships that* *produce desired results for the company."*

Question 75: How does your boss get the best out of you?

This is a rare question, but it's one that I always ask. It tells me as an interviewer how a job candidate likes to be managed. It also tells me how well the person will respond given the management I know he or she will be under. If you've done your homework, you already know these factors and you'll be able to match your "preferences" with the management style you know to expect from this company.

WORST ANSWER: Expressing the desire for independence when the firm is highly centralized, or any other trait you desire that doesn't match well with the company's culture or management style.

BEST ANSWER: Since you're one of the rare job candidates who has done their homework about the firm, its needs, wants, culture, and style, you'll be fantastically suited to know ahead of time how your personal preferences match with the company. If they don't match, why are you interviewing here? You'll only become frustrated and disillusioned.

Your answers could include a boss that challenges you, one that communicates well, one that builds respect and trust amongst the team or one that has a lot of experience. In any event, your answer must be what the company or your potential new boss currently offers.

Question 76: How do you get the best out of your boss?

My natural follow-up question always elicits a chuckle. What the interviewer is looking for is a measure of adaptability needed in all employees since all employees must adapt in some way to their boss's preferences. The employee who even attempts to "get the best out of their boss" is far above most other candidates. I always look for someone who tries to understand the stresses and pressures a boss endures.

WORST ANSWER: I just try to stay out of her way ...

BEST ANSWER: Getting the best out of someone means having their best interests at heart. If your boss succeeds, there's a pretty good chance you will as well.

Example: "I think it's important to remember that we're all human. My boss has a lot of strengths and she is very good at what she does. The best way I can help "get the best" out of her is to keep her informed, keep relevant information flowing to her, solve problems before she has to get involved, and do the best job I possibly can by [mention the most vital aspects and activities the open position demands]."

Question 77: What were your three most important responsibilities on your last job?

This appears to be a simple information gathering question, but many times it's followed up with "What special skills or knowledge did you need to perform those duties?" These two questions combine to give the interviewer a larger view of your functional background as well as an insight into your depth of understanding. If you've had any specialized training, this is a perfect time to mention it. It tells your interviewer that your previous employer felt you were a good investment of the time and money spent on training (this is an endorsement in and of itself). It also tells the interviewer that such an investment won't have to be made on his dime!

WORST ANSWER: Remember Question 2? Make certain your answer contains the responsibilities that match the job to which you're applying. It doesn't do any good to answer "ringing up customers, ordering product, and controlling inventory" if you're applying for an accounting job.

BEST ANSWER: Responsibilities that match your interviewer's greatest wants or needs will raise your value in the interviewer's eyes most. Since you've done your homework and know what those needs are, you're already ahead of the game. If you've recently graduated college with an accounting degree but your only experience was in working at Old Navy as a cashier, think about how your experience applies:

Example: "My top three responsibilities were to account for all cash, checks, and credit card receipts at the end of my shift and balance those with what our management information system calculated. I was responsible to audit the cycle counts of all merchandise in my area, and I also trained newcomers to the company."

See how those responsibilities match what an accounting firm might like to see? Always, always, always tailor your responses to match what your interviewer is looking for. Yes, he probably knows what you're doing, but the fact that you're already thinking like an employee and matching your former responsibilities to the ones demanded of the open position will prove you're the best candidate.

Question 78: When you managed others in previous positions, what was the average tenure of someone who resigned or quit to work elsewhere?

People often quit jobs no matter how good the management but what the interviewer is trying to uncover is whether your management style or your training ability is questionable. If the majority of people who quit while you were in charge did so relatively quickly, your training skills or willingness to adequately pay them could come into question. If, however, most people quit after a few years, chances are your management style will come into question.

WORST ANSWER: Anything specific. Blaming others for high turnover in your department is also a big no-no.

BEST ANSWER: The best way to answer this question is to be a bit vague and then reinforce your positive beliefs about how to manage people.

> *Example: "It varied, sometimes there would be people who would start but soon quit because their dream job opened, others would resign because they wanted more opportunity than was available at the time. I believe, however, that if you pay people reasonably, recognize their contributions consistently, publicly and in different ways, give them a decent work environment and a positive atmosphere, then resignations will naturally be very low. That is what I always strive for as a manager."*

Question 79: What makes you angry?

You don't want to come across as a pushover or a firebrand either. There's no value in being someone who overlooks everything nor in being the boss from hell. Neither is productive.

WORST ANSWER: A softball answer for a rigid, tough company or a feisty answer for a very cool, reserved firm.

BEST ANSWER: Your answer should be equally suited to your personality and the management style of the firm. Here, the homework you've done about the company and its style can help in your choice of words. Don't try to be something you're not. If the position calls for a tough minded, outspoken Attila the Hun type and you're more like Winnie the Pooh, you might as well keep looking. You wouldn't be happy anyway.

> *Example: If you're even tempered and the firm is stocked with ice cold professionals -- "I'm relatively calm and reserved and I believe those characteristics help me work with others and help me manage others within my department. If something isn't going well, my natural disposition is to find out why and get things back on track as quickly as possible. If there is not good reason, I will probably get impatient ... and even angry ... and I will take the necessary steps to insure that things of this nature won't happen again. However, I believe that if you hire right, compensate fairly, motivate well, and follow up consistently, things rarely get to that state."*

> *Example: If you're feisty by nature and the firm is stocked with hotheads -- "Know what makes me angry? People who won't do their jobs. Nothing frustrates me more than knowing that someone is capable but unwilling to go the distance for the company. OR people who lie and try to cover their own laziness. OR people who are always negative about company directives."*

Make certain you match your tendencies with the organizations culture.

Question 80: Have you ever experienced an employee or co-worker suddenly start acting out of character?

People problems do intrude upon the workplace. Whether drug problems, marital problems, or emotional problems, today's management team is expected to be on the lookout for these things since they could potentially affect production, morale, turnover, or the company's viability. The interviewer is looking for a caring attitude on your part because that character trait can go a long way toward increasing employee and co-worker loyalty. He is looking primarily for your sensitivity to privacy, sensitivity to the issue and the affected person, and delicacy in your answer.

WORST ANSWER: Since it's probably happened to everyone, the worst answer is going into detail about a situation with a previous employer. It can sound like gossip and no one likes to hear gossip in an interview. Another bad answer is to say that you made the decision of your own accord to set up counseling sessions for a co-worker or employee. That can lead to legal troubles.

BEST ANSWER: Walk on eggshells, thinking about -- every -- single -- word -- you -- say. Speak in generic terms (a co-worker was working through some personal issues) and never name names.

> *Example: "Yes, I have. I don't like to speak ill of anyone so I'm going to be very careful in how I choose my words here.[pause] I had an employee who was having some personal difficulties at home and those unfortunately spilled over into his professional life. I was concerned about his productivity, with so much going on in his personal life, so I asked if I could lighten his work load for a few days and he went ballistic on me. I just let him rant for a minute and calmly asked him to return to his workstation. At that point I went ahead and called Human Resources and apprised them of the situation. I called him back into my office two hours later and, with our HR director in the office, told him I thought he needed to take a few days off. It was Thursday and the next Monday was Labor Day so he wasn't going to miss much. Our HR department made him aware of some free counseling sessions and I believe he may have taken advantage of them because when he returned to work, he was back to his old self. I think the best thing to do in situations like this is to be understanding and caring and to make sure the employee knows that. I also believe it's important to never bring it up again."*

Question 81: All my other candidates have a college degree. Why should I hire you - considering you don't?

This is a common question, though rarely asked out loud. If it IS asked of you, make sure you're prepared. Giving the interviewer a "deer-in-the-headlights" look will almost certainly seal your fate, but a thoughtful answer could rescue your candidacy.

WORST ANSWER: My kids got in the way. I needed to start making money right out of high school. I got married too young. Anything that sounds like an excuse could be an interview killer.

BEST ANSWER: Acknowledge the validity of the interviewer's concern, then assure him that you have the skills and qualifications this position requires. Back up your claims with several specific examples that match HIS needs and you'll turn a potential interview killer into an interview booster.

> *Example: "That's a great question and I'm glad you asked. In today's business world, degrees are certainly one thing that I would want to consider if I were hiring, but they're only one of the aspects I would consider. I would want to insure that any candidate I was considering had skills and qualifications for the job. I think you can tell from my resume, and eventually my references, that my abilities, skills, and qualifications to [insert the jobs top requirement here] are exactly what this position needs. While I may not have a degree, I do have the skills and experience to help this firm achieve its goals and objectives. [give specific examples addressing the interviewer's highest priorities as you understand them]."*

Question 82: Why aren't you earning more money at this stage in your career?

Tough question. The interviewer is basically asking why you haven't been as successful paycheck-wise as the average person with your level of experience. Make sure you don't give the impression that money isn't important to you, yet you want to explain why your salary may be a little below industry standards

WORST ANSWER: Claims of bias or unfairness in past performance reviews or claiming that money isn't all that important.

BEST ANSWER: Making money is only one of your priorities when selecting a job.

> *Example: "Making money is a very important aspect of work, I agree. After all, this isn't a volunteer position and one reason I'm sitting here today is because I'm looking to make more. That being said, money is only one of my priorities. Others include liking my company, being able to work with top notch professionals I respect, and being able to maintain a work-life balance that gives me time with my family. As a matter of fact, my ideal position would be one where [match your ideal job as closely as possible to the position you're interviewing for].*

Question 83: Have you ever considered becoming an entrepreneur and starting your own company?

Answer YES excitedly and a large company will see you as a fire-brand. On the other side of the coin, a small company may fear you'll strike out on your own, taking their customers and trade secrets. Answer no and you could come across as a security minded dullard who never had a dream.

WORST ANSWER: Yes or no can sink your candidacy. The last thing you want to project is an image of either a dreamer who failed and is now settling for the corporate safety net ...or a restless maverick that will secretly sneak out the door with key accounts, contacts, and trade secrets under his arms just as soon as he can find the capital to fund his own start-up.

BEST ANSWER: The best answer can only be crafted after you've done your homework. You simply MUST know and understand the company culture. Remember, you CAN be honest, but you don't have to tell the interviewer everything you've ever done or thought about concerning any entrepreneurial bent you may have. In either case, no matter what the company culture, if you truly want this position, be sure to indicate that any desires about running your own show are part of your past, not your present or future.

If the company is large or highly structured:

> *Example: "I've thought about it a few times, dreamed about it really (who hasn't), but most of my career successes have been within a corporate structure like yours. That's where I excel and where I can make my biggest and best contribution.*

If the company is small or free-spirited:

> *Example: "I believe, at this company, I can enjoy the best of both worlds. Here, I believe I would get the excitement of seeing ideas and plans take shape and combined with the resources and stability of a well-established organization, it sounds like the perfect environment for long-term success."*

Either way, match what you want with what the position offers. The more information you've discovered about the position and the company, the more believable your case.

Question 84: What motivates you to do your best on the job?

This is a personal question that only you can answer but it's best to think about it beforehand and be prepared. Don't get too specific, but deal in generalities. If you're pressed for specifics, use examples that match what the company does best in it's field.

WORST ANSWER: Specific, non-relevant answers such as pizza Fridays, a "big" bonus, a fat paycheck. The reason these aren't good answers is because pizza isn't relevant, bonuses are earned, and a fat paycheck can be relative.

BEST ANSWER: Remember the C.A.R. method -- Challenge, Achievement, Recognition. Craft your answers around those three elements within the parameters of the company's strengths and you'll give the interviewer the exact answer he wants to hear.

> *Example: "Several things motivate me. A challenging position is one, a position that keeps me on the cutting edge of my skills and abilities and*

causes me to grow professionally. Another is a sense of getting something done that needed doing, achievement if you will. The third is being recognized for my work. As I understand this company, the challenge is exactly what I crave in [the open position] and I believe my skills would insure high level of success and achievement. Given how you reward your employees, I believe you'd find me to be among one of your most motivated employees."

Question 85: Can you explain your career progression from [position A] to [position B]? It appears to me that you took a step backwards. Is that true?

Interviewers consider a career in terms of "progression," and progress only knows one direction: UP. If you're asked this question, it probably means that your interviewer doesn't understand why you would accept a position as a store manager when you were previously a district manager. He could be wondering why your progress came to a screeching halt and if you're capable of starting it back again. Taking a lesser position won't necessarily derail your interview or career, as long as you are smart about how you present the experience - and the reasons for it - to your interviewer. Always remember: you aren't marketing the skills and abilities from your last job(s), you're marketing the unique set of skills, education, and experiences that you can bring to the table that will help solve your interviewer's most pressing problems.

WORST ANSWER: Allowing yourself to be blindsided by this question, becoming defensive or curt with your answer.

BEST ANSWER: Your goal is to make a lesser position sound interesting and worthwhile to your interviewer. Interviewers want to see employees that are actively engaged with their work, even if the position wasn't their first choice. Such employees will usually be more appealing to employers, especially when interviewing for the kind of job that will be a much better fit. Your goal is to emphasize the strengths you posses that will be invaluable to the company and the fact that NO position is worthless.

Example: "I took that position for several reasons, and I quickly learned how valuable it was. It opened my eyes to [operations, accounting, etc] and I learned a great deal about how that department/position fits within the company. I believe that learning opportunities are everywhere, and it's important to continue to move forward even when you aren't in your ideal career position. Looking back, I wouldn't change anything."

Question 86: What steps could you have taken to improve your career progress?

This isn't the question you think it is. It really is just a variation of Question 30 or Question 65 -- designed to get you to confess a regret. The question really is, "If you could, how would you live your life over?" No one wins by living in the past, only by learning from it, so don't fall for any such invitations to rewrite personal history. You can't win if you do.

WORST ANSWER: Answering the question at face value. We all have regrets (whether we confess them to others or not), but answering this question improperly can make you appear tepid, fearful, and regretful.

BEST ANSWER: Express general satisfaction with your career progress. There are always things you wish you had known or had foreseen, such as the booming growth in a particular field or corporate downsizing that would phase out your last position), but all things considered, you take full personal responsibility for where you are in your career, how you arrived there, where you are heading. Most of all, harbor no regrets and never blame anyone else for where you are today.

Question 87: What is more important to you: the money or the work?

Money is always important, but the work you perform is the most important. Every employee who has quit a job in frustration knows the importance of enjoying their line of work. let's face it, there ARE a few positions that you wouldn't do no matter the salary. Watched any episodes of *Dirty Jobs* recently?

WORST ANSWER: This question may be posed to you in different ways, at different times in the interview. The interviewer knows what he's doing: he's looking for inconsistent answers on your part to determine if you've been coached or have read an eBook on interviewing. The worst thing you could do is answer differently than you did before.

BEST ANSWER: The best answer is to put things into perspective. Money IS important -- highly important -- after all, no one works for free, but enjoying what your work, your co-workers, and boss rank higher. We all know people, perhaps you've been in this same circumstance, who were highly paid but despised their job. You don't want to find yourself in that position but at the same time, you don't want to love your job but have to work 2 or 3 of them to put food on the table and live the lifestyle you want.

> *Example: "My honest answer is that it* depends *on the money and the work. Obviously there are positions I wouldn't do no matter the pay, but others I would consider on a volunteer basis. In reality, though, I don't think a strong compensation package and enjoyable work are mutually exclusive. My desire is to work in a field that offers me not only the challenge of growth and personal development, but professional development as well. Based on what I've learned about this open position at your company, I believe I'm an ideal fit."*

Question 88: Have you ever been in a crisis situation where things got out of control? How did you handle it?

In a mining disaster there are always those who will scream at the darkness and those who will keep their cool, find a working headlamp and lead the others to find a way out. You probably know people who would fit into either category but you can rest assured that your interviewer prefers someone who can handle any crisis in a levelheaded manner.

WORST ANSWER: A lack of preparedness can derail your interview very quickly should this question arise. You never want to appear panicked or unprepared.

BEST ANSWER: Your preparedness for this interview can work wonders should this question be one your interviewer uses. Your "pre-job" job is to know what types of crises typically surprise this company. For a retailer, it may be a supplier issue, but for a manufacturer, it may be equipment failure or union issues, while wholesalers face transportation issues. You have to know what challenges your interviewer's company faces and have a backup plan for handling them. You also want to emphasize what you learned and how you adapted.

> *Example: "In my last position I managed part of our supply chain and because of some competitive issues, we began using an overseas supplier in China. We started using them in the summer and everything was going quite well -- we were getting timely shipments and utilizing a just-in-time style of inventory management. That all went awry when Chinese New Year hit the following January. Our shipments were delayed six to eight weeks and our customers didn't really care about what was going on half-a-world away. Fortunately, I had maintained contact with a few of our stateside suppliers and was able to limp along until our overseas shipments arrived. The following October, I ordered double what I would have normally ordered and we were able to easily supply our customers through the Spring. The downside to that year was that our profit took a minor hit because of the increased costs from stateside suppliers and the double orders in the fall of that year, but the following year we were able to rebound very nicely and we surpassed our divisional profit goal by 28 percent."*

Question 89: Tell me how you plan your day/week/month.

This is a straightforward time management question and many interviewers use it. Your interviewer is looking for a candidate that understands the principles of time management and puts them into practice daily. What are those principles or habits?

> 1. The habit of setting aside time each day or week to plan --

whether at the beginning or at the end of the day or week.
2. The habit of prioritizing those plans -- deciding what is most important, what is second, what is third, and so on.
3. The habit of putting those plans into motion and sticking to them -- essentially, not getting distracted by busywork, rather focusing on the important task at hand.
4. The habit of reviewing each day's activities to see where you need to adapt tomorrow's plans -- then going back to step #1.

WORST ANSWER: As usual, no plan is a bad plan. Don't ever think that "flexibility" will trump a well thought out plan. You may have to adapt at some point, but claiming that you "wing it" won't score any points.

BEST ANSWER: If you use a calendar system, mention it, but the main thing is to adapt your answer to the interviewer's needs. Many people refer to the four steps mentioned above as the Plan-Do-Review cycle and virtually every position could benefit from its use. Even police officers, whose days are never the same, plan where to patrol, what or who to look for, and when to complete their paperwork.

> *Example: "I take 15 minutes every morning and think about what needs to be done and write those items on a legal pad (or calendar). Then I decide what needs to be done first or what is the most important thing on that list by asking, 'If I could ONLY do one thing today, what would it be?', then 'If I could ONLY do two things today, what would they be?' Then I get to work on my list. I know things will come up that are unexpected, so I calculate in a moderate amount of flexibility into my schedule. Then, at the end of the day, I take a few minutes to evaluate what happened, how I did, and where I can improve. Those few minutes at the end of the day help me plan the next day as well."*

Question 90: If it were offered to you, would you like to have your boss' job?

The interviewer you're facing may be your future boss and this question may be one designed to determine if you're a potential threat down the road. Most professionals don't mind someone snapping at their heels as long as it's driving them up the corporate ladder but blind ambition from someone below you is irritating. It also makes many interviewers wonder if the candidate will stab them in the back in order to get promoted.

WORST ANSWER: The worst answer is yes -- especially if you're not yet qualified, over-qualified, or if you come across as overly ambitious.

BEST ANSWER: If the true answer is yes, make certain you assure your interviewer that you're interested in professional development that results in advancement and that the best way to advance is to push someone from the bottom because of the results you produced. If you've done your homework, you already know what results the company craves and you'll be able to adapt your answer to the company's needs. Be sure to mention that you would only want that position if it were a good fit for you and if you were ready to assume that role.

If your answer is no, don't come right out and say it. Tiptoe around the answer by, again, saying that you're interested in professional development and producing the results that would cause your advancement within the company. You believe in merit promotions and you're eager to begin proving your worth and producing the kind of results this company desires.

Question 91: Sell me this pen (pencil, stapler, adding machine, desk, clock, etc).

The real question is: *do you understand the sales process and can you sell?* If your interviewer is a business owner or a hard-changing executive in a marketing driven company, he may place a high importance on each job candidate's ability to sell, regardless of which position you're interviewing for. These entrepreneurs are overly focused on the sales process, but you can turn even that to your advantage. Be ready if your homework has revealed that your interviewer could be one of these executives.

WORST ANSWER: If you've never been in a sales position before, you'll be blindsided by this challenging question and unpreparedness is a big negative.

BEST ANSWER: The most important secret of any great sales person is this: *Ask questions to determine your prospect's needs, then show him or her* *how to meet those needs.*

You've been selling yourself for the entire interview already, so if your interviewer holds up his pen and challenges you to sell it to him, simply demonstrate that you know and understand that most important secret.

Example: "A good salesperson knows both his product and his prospect before he sells anything so first I'd get to know everything I could about the pen, its features, benefits, warranties, and options. Then I would ask some questions to determine your needs such as, 'Just out of curiosity, if you didn't already have a pen like this, why would you want one? And in addition to that? Any other reason? Anything else? Why do you say that?' and I would wait and listen to your answers. I would go on by asking, 'And would you want your pen to be reliable?... Write smoothly without leaving smudges? ... Would you prefer a cap or a clicking pen?' Then I would present all the features and benefits of this pen and why it's exactly what the you just told me you were looking for. I would begin to close by asking, 'Just out of curiosity, what would you consider a reasonable price for a quality pen like this...a pen you could have right now and would do everything you just told me was important? No matter his number, (unless it's zero), say, 'Excellent! You just bought the exact pen you need.'" If he does say ZERO, begin asking for referrals.

Your interviewer may fight with you, denying he wants the pen or challenge your assertions about it. Whatever you do, don't fight back. Take the pen away from him and say, "Mr. Interviewer, I'm happy to know upfront that there's no way you'd ever want this pen. As you know, the most important rule of selling is to uncover and meet the needs of people who really need and want our products. Doing so otherwise just wastes everyone's time and I certainly would not want to waste your time. But since my firm has many different items that could potentially meet your other needs do you see anything on this desk that you would like to own?" After he points something out, repeat your question and answer process and make an alternate presentation like I mentioned above. If your interviewer knows anything about sales, he will be very impressed.

Question 92: Can you forget your education and start from scratch?

Your interviewer may not put much stock in education or may ask this question to shock you. He may be using it to create turmoil or shock to gage your self-control in a confusing situation. Interviewers may also use this question (or one like it) to flush out an aggression problem or as an early warning for those exhausting times when a manager has to deal with someone who "knows-it-all" but has zero business sense or experience.

WORST ANSWER: Attitude is the biggest problem here. If you've been asked this question, it's time to back down about your education.

BEST ANSWER: Adaptability to what the interviewer needs will diffuse any concern that you're relying solely on your education. Take the time to point out that your education was just the foundation and with a sound foundation, you can build any type, size, or style of home you like. The same holds true for your education -- it was just the beginning of your professional growth and you hope to continue that growth by helping this company meet its needs and objectives.

Question 93: Did you hold any budgetary responsibilities in your last position?

Many executives claim that managers without fiscal responsibilities aren't managers at all. They're nothing more than order takers or straw bosses. Regardless, the level of a manager's fiscal responsibility and his or her ability to manage it effectively is a sure benchmark used to judge a candidate's true capability for handling money and budgets.

WORST ANSWER: Surprise or unpreparedness for this question is the worst answer, but downplaying the importance of budgetary responsibilities is also undesirable.

BEST ANSWER: Specifics. Outline exactly what your budgetary responsibilities were in your last position and how they affected the department and the company. Take it a step further by relaying how, based on your research about the position, you would be able to effectively produce this company's desired results because of your experience. Even if the budget is larger, reiterate how your career progression would naturally lead to this open position

Question 94: What methods have you used in past performance reviews?

Your interviewer is looking for a systematic approach to your use of personnel evaluations. Your interviewer wants to see that you were fair and consistent in how you held people accountable for their performance.

WORST ANSWER: A flippant answer is the worst. Also high on the DO NOT list is anything that appears like you just "winged it."

BEST ANSWER: Emphasize your logical and consistent approach to personnel evaluations against measured, clearly communicated, objective, and predetermined performance criteria. Follow up with a question asking how this company reviews and evaluates the performance if its employees. If you've done your homework, you already know, but it is a great follow up question to ask your interviewer.

> *Example: "I don't like to evaluate anyone unless they know what's expected of them, so I begin each year by laying out our corporate goals and objectives for each person, making certain I communicate that these goals aren't written in stone and they may need to be adapted to changing market conditions. I also insist that the employee 'buys-in' to these goals and that he or she has an active voice in the steps needed to take to achieve them. Then I periodically check up on each employee to see if they need any help reaching their goals throughout the year. At the end of the year, annual performance reviews are rarely surprising."*

Question 95: Would you be willing to fill in for someone with lower-level responsibilities for an extended period of time?

This questions goes to the heart of any candidate's flexibility and adaptability. Answer the wrong way and you'll appear to be a   prima-donna, but answer like the team player you are and you'll set yourself up to score some serious points with your interviewer.

WORST ANSWER: No. Any other answer that makes you appear to be inflexible or unwilling to participate as a team player. Another poor answer is, "It depends." It makes your willingness conditional and makes you come across as a diva.

BEST ANSWER: Yes! Of course. Sure. Then follow up with something like, "How often does this type of situation occur?" Chances are this was just a test question, but there are many times that firms need flexible people to fill in (temporarily) for another employee who may be on vacation, on jury duty, or tied up with a special project.

Let's face it. There are times when a boss needs someone to patch a weakness in another department or cover for someone who's out on leave for whatever reason. Your willingness to be the "go to" person for your boss will make you out to be the hero. We all live an work in dynamic environments and a strict adherence to a job description eliminates your ability to prove your worth through flexibility.

Question 96: What has been the most expensive fiscal mistake of your career?

Careful. We DO NOT rehash old history or opine about what might have been. That being said, this question could be a great opportunity for you to shine.if you answer it correctly. The important thing to remember is that any mistake can result in great things if you learned something.

WORST ANSWER: Denying that you ever made a mistake, or answering the question without going into detail about what you learned.

BEST ANSWER: Since no one is perfect, pick a mistake that wasn't too expensive to learn. One option is to tell a story about not speaking up when your boss was making a financial mistake or, if you did speak up, your mistake was not being forceful enough with your boss or upper management. Always follow up by telling the interviewer what you learned and then tell a story that proves you learned those lessons.

Example: "I'm careful when it comes to my own money and doubly so when I'm in charge of my company's money. I try very diligently to avoid making mistakes in the first place, but no one's perfect. In my last position, I made the mistake of over-ordering promotional T-Shirts for our company's charity marathon. Basically, I ordered too many small and medium sized shirts and while I had plenty of the sizes we did need, those five boxes were a constant reminder that I didn't double check the order. After I realized what I did and that those shirst weren't doing us any good, I received permission to donate them to the local youth home and to a local school that we supported. The next time I placed a similar order, I was very careful to double and triple check my order and we had just the right amount."

Question 97: Tell me how you organize and plan for major projects.

Interviewers want to know if you have a sensible approach to planning or if you'll need someone to hold your hand and nurse you along when the big project comes down the pike. No interviewer wants to overlook the importance of hiring someone who knows and understands the planning process and is able to effectively implement it.

WORST ANSWER: A blank stare. Possibly even worse is the fact that you were unprepared for such a question.

BEST ANSWER: Make certain your interviewer knows that you use a logical approach to planning and executing major projects. You typically start with the project's goals and timeline. From there you work backwards to determine milestones and potential bottlenecks. You build your milestone schedule with beginning and ending dates for each component part of the project and include a breakdown of human resource utilization as well as any contingencies. You identify budget resources and insure that your projects are completed on time and under budget.

The natural follow up question will be: "Tell me about your latest project and how you used these steps." You better be ready because you just were called on the carpet.

Question 98: The crazy question.

"Why are manhole covers round?" was a question supposedly asked at Microsoft by Bill Gates. Whether this was true or not, interviewers will often ask a crazy sounding question with a straight face just to watch the candidate squirm.Sometimes called "Stump the Chump" by HR folks, these questions are designed to see if you can think on your feet. Make sure you Google a couple of these questions so you're not totally unprepared.

WORST ANSWER: Acting like you know what you're talking about when you don't or tapping on your iPhone to get the answer.

BEST ANSWER: If you don't know, concede that point, but don't try to make up a professional sounding answer. Educated guesses are okay, they demonstrate to your interviewer that you're thinking about the answer. I've used this exact question on many interviews and the responses are usually quite revealing. A "know-it-all" will feign knowledge about everything from the way sewers are shaped to the expense involved in manufacturing manhole covers. I don't want to hire a "know-it-all." A better response is a simple *I don't know, but I'll do some research and find out.* I would much rather hire someone who can admit their lack of knowledge and commit to finding the answer. And finding the answer at a later date gives you the opportunity to call your interviewer back!

The reason manhole covers are round is so they won't fall back into the sewer since other shapes can be maneuvered to fit back into the manhole.

Question 99:   Where do you see yourself six months (or one/five/ten years from now)?

This is a corporate ladder vs clock watcher question and you already know which one the interviewer wants. If you're seeking a career path, here is your opportunity to speak up but be careful. Many candidates use this question as an opportunity to showcase their ambition but you can easily come across as a wanna-be. The answers I've been given to this question over the years have ranged from a blank stare (with "I -- don't -- know...) to the classic yet mildly offensive and bold: "I want YOUR job." I don't typically hire either of these people.

WORST ANSWER: "I don't know. I. Just. Don't. Know." was the worst I've ever heard and it smacked of zero ambition, though the person who told me this used his father's connections to get hired anyway.   Grrr.

BEST ANSWER: The best answer is one that shows the interviewer you're ambitious, but you're willing to put in all the work, training, seasoning, education, and hours necessary to succeed. You HAVE to know what it takes to reach your goal, otherwise you could be labeled a "dreamer."

Question 100:   Do you have any questions for me?

You better. No interview covers everything and any interviewee should have at least three or four specific questions that are pertinent to the position.

WORST ANSWER:"   No, you've covered everything very well." Another poor question is to immediately launch into a series of questions on benefits, vacation days, sick days, health insurance, etc.

BEST ANSWER: Having questions that naturally relate to the position are best but if none immediately come to mind try asking:

1. About a typical day in the position, the volume of work, the pace of the work or the person you'll be reporting to.
2. The interviewer how he or she came to work for the company. Lean forward and show some interest.
3. About the company culture (you should already know, but it demonstrates your interest in the position).

When I interview potential candidates for a position, few things irritate me like an applicant who never asks any questions about the company or the position. When a candidate is engaged, asks specific questions, and even takes notes, I take note as well! It shows interest in the position and makes me think they're probably going to perform well.

When the questions coming from your interviewer start to wane, take charge of the interview with some questions of your own.

1. Tell me about the exact nature of the job, who this position reports to, the responsibilities of the position, and the desired results.

2. Tell me about the boss' style of management.
3. What are the key targets or goals of the position?
4. How do you know you're succeeding?
5. What is essential for success in this position?
6. What in my background makes you think I'd be a good fit for this position?
7. What makes a good employee in this position?
8. What characteristics to you admire in your boss?
9. Why is the position open?
10. What happened to the last person who held this position (quit, promoted, fired, transferred, died, retired)?
11. Why is this a great job?
12. What growth is projected for the future regarding the company or the position?
13. Why is this a great job?

Interview the company as much as it's interviewing you.

You are a valuable commodity! You have a unique set of skills, education, experience, and insights. Any company who thinks you're worthy of an interview obviously saw something they liked. **Make sure you cultivate their interest by showing interest in them.**

The interviewer may decline to interest certain questions but even their declination can tell you something. For example, if you ask what happened to the person who formerly held the open position and you've already uncovered information that "he was invited to seek employment elsewhere," the interviewer may respond with, "He's no longer with us." At that point, you should ask whether the goals of the position were met or exceeded in previous years (or quarters). If the answer is no, you might wonder if the goals were actually attainable. Ask what those goals were. You need to know! If the answer is yes, it might indicate that the last person was offered a position with a competitor.

An interview is like a dance and dancing is a lot more fun when someone is doing it with you. Dancing alone while someone watches you isn't a lot of fun so – participate! Join in the fun. **Ask questions of your interviewer.** Don't be afraid to ask about how they came to be employed with the company and take a few notes.

The Illegal Question

Illegal questions include any question about:

1. your age
2. Number and ages of your children or other dependents
3. Your plans to have children
4. Marital status
5. Maiden name
6. Religion
7. Political affiliation
8. Ancestry
9. National origin
10. Birthplace
11. Naturalization of your parents, spouse or children
12. Diseases
13. Disabilities
14. Cubs
15. Spouse's occupation
16. Arrests

... unless any of the above **are directly related to your performance of the job.** If it's an important part of your job function, you can be asked. When it comes to arrests, though you can't be asked about them, you <u>can</u> be asked about convictions. All this can vary by state or country so check with an attorney for verification. Laws change all the time.

Under the ever-present threat of lawsuits, most interviewers are keenly aware of these boundaries. But you may run into someone, typically a senior executive, who doesn't interview much and forgets he can't ask such questions. Mostly this happens   usually on a second or third interview and the Human Resources person in the room will probably panic and ask for a moment with the executive.

What if you're asked an illegal question? Your first option is to assert your legal right not to answer. This rarely works to your benefit and may even frighten or embarrass your interviewer. Any rapport you had built to this point will likely be destroyed.

Your next option is to get over your fears about privacy and answer the question. Sometimes answering can help you. For example, if you discover that your interviewer is a new parent (you found out through research and by the shrine in her office), you could gain by talking about your love of children and desire to have them.

Lastly, and probably the best approach if you don't want your privacy invaded, is to tactfully address the interviewer's concern that's hiding behind the question without answering the illegal question directly.

Examples:

Illegal question: *"How old are you?"*
Your best answer: "Is there some concern that my age could impact my performance? I can assure you that there is nothing about this job that I can't do and considering the wealth of experience I bring to the table I can [insert your plan to meet the interviewer's greatest needs].

Illegal question: *"Do you plan to have children?"*
Your best answer: "I am wholeheartedly dedicated to my career, and though I love children, I have no plans for them." (Don't worry, your plans can change. Just get the job first and then enjoy all your options.)

Illegal question: *"That's an Irish last name, isn't it?"*
Your best answer: "That depends on whether St. Patrick's day is a company holiday!" Smiling, of course.

Sometimes illegal questions bloom out of small talk but some arise from fear that you won't perform well. Your best answer of all is to get the job and perform brilliantly. All concerns and fears will then varnish, replaced by respect and admiration for your contribution to the company.

The "Hidden" Illegal Question

Much more frequent than the Illegal question is the hidden illegal question. Why is it called the "hidden" illegal question? Because it isn't asked out loud, it's asked only in the interviewer's mind. These are the questions that are most damaging and since you don't have the opportunity to address them, you may never get the chance you need to prove your worth.

You may be over 50, or a single mother returning to your professional career, or physically challenged, or a member of a minority, or maybe born in another country, or don't perfectly fit into the definition of "normal" for this company. Your interviewer may wonder, "Is this person really able to handle the job?"…"Is he or she a 'good fit' at a place like ours?"…"Will the chemistry ever be right with someone like this?" But the interviewer never raises such questions because they're illegal. So what can you do?

Remember that just because the interviewer doesn't ask an illegal question doesn't mean he doesn't have it. More than likely, he is going to come up with his own answer. So you might as well help him out. How? Well, you obviously can't respond to an illegal question if he   hasn't even asked. This may well offend him. And there's always the chance he   wasn't even concerned about the issue until you brought it up, and only then begins to wonder.

So you can't address "hidden" illegal questions head-on. But what you can do is make sure there's enough counterbalancing information to more than reassure him that there's no problem in the area he may be doubtful about.

For example, let's say you had an accident as a child and you need a cane to walk. You know your condition has never caused a performance issue, but you're still concerned that your interviewer may secretly be wondering about your stamina or ability to travel. Make sure that you emphasize these abilities several times, leaving no doubt about your capacity to handle them well.

It's a shame that we still have these biases, so if you're in any way different from what passes as "normal," make certain, without seeming defensive, that you mention strengths, accomplishments, preferences and affiliations that strongly counterbalance any unspoken concern your interviewer may have.

Background Checks

Background checks are becoming more common these days as employers strive to insure that they're getting everything that's been advertised in a candidate. If you're like me, you'd much rather know what someone will see in that background check than get surprised. To make sure neither you nor your potential employer are surprised, take these steps:

1.   **Order your credit report.** It costs nothing to use Annual Credit Report.com and you can get one each year free of charge from each of the three credit bureaus. It really is the first step in preparing for a background check. If there is anything you don't recognize or that you disagree with, dispute the information in writing (certified mail) with the creditor and/or credit bureau before you have to explain it to the interviewer. It's a good idea to get your credit report each year anyway to help detect identity theft. Inaccurate information will be removed but negative information that's true will not.

2.   **Look at old background checks.** If you've been the subject of a previous background check, you may be legally entitled to receive a copy from the employment screening company. If you don't know the name of the company performing the background check, ask the employer who requested the investigation. Of course there probably   isn't anything in there if that employer hired you, but it could give you some insight into what is included in a background check.

3.   **Check your DMV records.** Request a copy of your driving record from your state's Department of Motor Vehicles, especially if you are applying for a job that involves driving. A thorough background check always includes driving records.

4.   **Ask to see your personnel file from your old jobs.** State law might enable you to see your personnel file – even if you don't work for that employer anymore. For example, under California law, you can access your file until a year from the last date of employment, and you are allowed to make copies of documents in your file that have your signature on them. Ask your former employer if there is a policy about the release of personnel records. Many companies limit the amount of information they disclose.

5. **Check court records yourself.** If you already know you have an arrest record or if you've been involved in *any* court cases, physically go to the county courthouse where the records are stored and ask to inspect those files. Make sure the information is correct and up to date. Reporting agencies have been known to report felony convictions when the defendant truly believes the crime was reduced to a misdemeanor. *Court records are not always updated correctly.* If the needed signature to reduce the charges wasn't obtained or wasn't recorded by the court, those inaccurate records could thwart your employment plans. *Don't rely on what an attorney may have told you.* If you think the conviction was expunged or dismissed, get a certified copy from the court saying so.

6. **Do it yourself background check.** If you have a friend who can sound professional on the phone, ask him or her to act as an HR manager and call your job references, your old employers, old colleagues, and even your neighbors to see what they will say. Sneaky? Sure, but what gets revealed might surprise you. This is potentially dangerous so be careful.

1. Clean your digital room. Search your name, in quotations, on all the major search engines to see what comes up. If you find anything objectionable, contact the website to ask how to get it removed. I've had people make comments on my blog and later ask me to remove them because they were coming up in searches!

2. Read your Facebook, MySpace, Twitter, or other social networking profiles from your potential employer's perspective. Have you written something that puts your previous employer in a bad light? Have you mentioned that you're sick and tired of your boss? Have you said that you plan to quit your job? Remove or edit postings that could damage your job-seeking efforts. Don't remove content that shines a light on your positive achievements, though. If you've been listed as a volunteer or if your race times in the United Way's 10k Run are listed, those could actually help!

Many times, companies will ask you to submit to a background check when you fill out the application.

The background check authorization has to be on a separate form.

The only other information this form can include is your signature and information that identifies you such as a Social Security or driver's license number. No form in the application process is allowed to ask questions like "race," "sex," "full date of birth," or "maiden name." Such questions violate the Federal Equal Employment Opportunity laws. And, you should NEVER sign any document that waives your right to sue a screening company or the employer for violations of the law.

Business Dress

A few decades ago, the rules of business dress were simple: two or three piece business suits for men and women were expected to dress in a professional suit with a tea-length dark skirt with a jacket and buttoned up blouse. In recent years, the dress codes at many companies have relaxed, allowing employees to choose (within reason) what to wear to work. At many companies the dress code has become "dressy casual" – khakis and dress or golf shirts for men and women. Most employees welcome the freedom to wear something other than a dark suit, but it does require some discernment.

When going on an interview, make certain you find out what style of dress is appropriate. How? Ask. If you're using a recruiter, it's easy to ask him or her to shed some insight on what's acceptable. Otherwise, take a shot in the dark by calling the receptionist, asking what appropriate dress for an interview is. Chances are good you'll get the right answer. Increase the chances that you'll get it right by calling more than one person or department.

Business Dress Basics

Although there's no longer one single standard of business dress, there are still general guidelines you should follow:

- **Follow the dress code:** Many workplaces have abandoned written dress codes. Instead, observe the people around you and try to dress in a similar fashion. You can play James Bond 007 and stake out the company at 5pm to see what everyone is wearing.
- **Subtlety is the best policy:** Creativity is great, but if your clothing makes you stand out too much in an interview, your interviewer might interpret it that you don't respect the company or its culture. Unless you work in a very progressive field, visible tattoos and multiple piercings could also be a problem.
- **Dress slightly better than you should:** Dress as if you already have the job you want to get. Looking the part will help the interviewer imagine you in the position already..
- **Look tidy:** Style and trim your hair (including facial hair), keep your nails clean, and don't wear clothes with wrinkles or holes.
- **Limit makeup and cologne:** Too much makeup can make you look fake, while too much perfume or cologne can be overpowering and unpleasant.

- **Cover up:** Avoid tight, short, low-cut, or revealing clothes. They have no place in a professional interview.

Traditional Business Attire

If your interviewing in an office where the dress code is traditional, you should dress accordingly. In general, the fields of finance, healthcare, insurance, and law are more traditional, while entertainment, media, fashion, publicity, and technology are less so..

And you can always remove your tie or jacket if you've overdressed.

10 Quick Cover Letter Tips

Cover letters

1. Follow the instructions: If you're responding to an ad, provide *exactly* what's requested. If an online ad requests no attachments, don't send any. Give the company what they want and no more. If the ad requests job reference number, employment availability date and salary requirements, give them (give a salary range if required).

2. Know you're trying to reach: Research your company and tailor your letter to the open position's listed requirements. If you can find out who the boss is, tailor your cover letter to his or her needs in the department. Make every letter unique for the industry, the company, and the position.

3. Use a formal tone: Make sure you come across as thoughtful, responsible, and employable. Avoid overuse of "I" or "my" since the intent of your cover letter is to focus on the employer's requirements and how you can meet them. Some personal pronoun use is expected, just don't overdo it.

4. Use a traditional font and paper: Use a classic font, such as Times New Roman, Arial, Verdana, or Georgia on white or off-white 8.5"×11" paper. Anything else reeks of unprofessionalism unless you're in a creative field.

5. Keep it short: What do you want this cover letter to do? You want it to get you an interview! Long letters don't do that. Your goal should be to make it easy for a prospective employer to read your cover letter. If you make it too long, employers might not read it all.

6. Avoid unrelated personal information: Unless one of your hobbies relates to the job, don't mention your private life, political views, marital status, where you went on vacation, how many children you have, or your religion.

7. Give personal information that matters: That includes your name, address, phone numbers (home and cell) and a professional email address.

8. Use a professional email address: Using something like sexykitten@whatever.com or beerdrinkingfool@whatever.com won't cut it. Use something with your full name in it if possible.

9. Proofread: Proofreading is more than just a click of the spell-checker. You want readability. You want proper grammar. You want sentences that make sense and don't ramble. Read your letter aloud to see how it sounds, then have someone else read it to you and critique it. You don't want the HR department to be the first to critique your cover letter!

10. Sign your cover letter: Unless you're a doctor, make sure your signature is legible.

9 Quick Resume Tips

1. Start strong: Chances are good that your resume will be scanned by either a machine or human eyes. Make sure it starts strong with your highest and best achievements near the beginning. Use strong headlines (Significant Accomplishments, Transferable Skills, etc) to further enhance your resume's strength.

2. Accuracy reigns: Every detail in your resume must be 100% true and factual. Potential employers will check those details at some point. Count on it. They may not check today, but resume inaccuracies have a nasty habit of showing up years later. You don't want to use this eBook to get your dream job only to get fired for exaggerating your accomplishments on a resume.

3. Get to the point: Your résumé should fit on one page unless you have extensive work experience (more than 10 years), in which case it can be two pages … at most. People just don't read resumes longer than two pages.

4. List skills, not just positions held: Skills are as important as job titles, perhaps even more so. Describe your skills and accomplishments as specifically as possible, using strong, active verbs.

5. Quantify your achievements: Don't just list your achievements, quantify them whenever possible. For example, "Increased sales" versus "Increased sales 35% in the second quarter of 2010" - see the difference? Use phrases that match the job description's requirements such as "Cut production and labor costs resulting in savings of $40,000 per month" or "Instituted a customer tracking and response program that doubled the number of customers within one year."

6. Use relevant keywords: Many resumes are scanned into large databases and guess what they're looking for? Keywords. Integrate keywords that match the open position's description into the entire document to make your resume stand out in these electronic searches.

7. Don't forget the basics: Include your name, address, phone number, and that professional email address I mentioned above.

8. Control yourself : Don't include information about your educational credentials (GPA, test scores, etc.) unless you've graduated in the past five years. Photos and detailed personal information are also unnecessary in the United States, but in many European, Latin American and Asian countries, photos are expected.

9. Proofread: Grammatical or formatting mistakes on your résumé make you look careless.

About the Author

Ron Haynes majored in Human Resources Management in undergraduate school and later went to graduate school to earn an MBA. He has started several very successful businesses, including a restaurant and a lumberyard. Although the buyers of the restaurant eventually shut it down, the lumberyard is still thriving.

After selling his shares of the lumberyard, he went on to become a partner with a large holding company having retail stores over 140 locations spread across 15 states. It currently is ranked as one of the top 20 firms in its industry.

Bonus Worksheet 1 – The Company's Needs Analysis

How to uncover your interviewer's greatest need(s).

Write the job description of the open position:

____

____

____

____

Now CIRCLE any keywords that stand out. Bear in mind that many Human Resources departments now list the requirements for each position as essential, needed, and/or bonus (sort of a must have, need to have, and would be nice).

If the position was assistant manager and you found this job description on the company's website or it was given to you:

> *Operate as a "Working Manager." A Working Manager is an individual that gets involved in the daily activities and performs any job duties necessary to keep the store operating at maximum efficiency.*

> *Effectively manage partners, personally and through other supervisors, at Barton's location in order to maximize profitability, control costs, and offer the best possible customer service.*

> *Continually exceed high levels of profitability and customer service while making certain the store is following all safety regulations, guidelines, and operating procedures.*

In this example, I would circle working manager, efficiency, manage, maximize profitability, customer service, and safety.

Now, how do you stack up? What have you done in the past that demonstrates these skills? Which jobs did you perform these vital functions exceptionally well? What were the circumstances? What in your personal makeup causes you to function at a high level with these particular capacities?

Think about those questions and write your answers by hand:

____

____

____

____

____

____

____

____

Who do you know that works in this industry or for this particular company? (refer to Bonus Worksheet 3) Ask if they have any knowledge about the functions of this open position. Would you be good at it? Why? Ask!

Ask your contact about the challenges this position represents. You're going to have to know this information before you walk into that interview and the more you know, the more you'll be able to tailor your answers, experiences, education, and skills to the interviewer's greatest need.

Perform a search engine query on the company and the position. Find out what other companies in the industry expect of the position. Read all the news you can possibly find on the company, especially as it relates to the open position. Take copious notes and memorize them. Your knowledge of the company could be the tipping point that nets you the job offer.

Bonus Worksheet 2 – Success Factors

Success Factor Analysis

The purpose of this worksheet is to help you uncover what areas of work that mean the most to you, what areas make you WANT to go to work. These are the elements, skills, and talents that enable you to bridge from one type of position to another or from one career to another. They will also help you plan for any future education (seminars, workshops, or other types of training) that will best help you in the growth and fulfillment of your career goals.

Instructions

Look over the worksheet first. In the left column there are talents, and skills that you may have used in your last ten major achievements, projects, or jobs. For your most recent achievement, project, of job, use number One, for the achievement, project, or job previous to that, use number Two and so on.

If you were required to be adaptable in your most recent achievement, put an X in the box intersecting Adapted and 1. If you were required to perform analysis, put an X in the box intersecting Analyzed and 1, and so on. Go all the way through the list and don't be shy. If you used the Success Factor in any way in accomplishing the achievement or position, mark the appropriate box.

You may check 20 or 30 Success Factors which contributed to the success of each of your ten achievements. Some of these undoubtedly contributed more than others. Now go down through the column of the worksheet for each achievement and circle the X of at least eight, but no more than ten Success Factors that contributed most. Total the number of circled X's and write it in the far right hand column.

Once you've performed this exercise, go across the rows and write in the space below the names of each Success Factor which has three or more circled X's.

____

____

____

____

____

____

These Success Factors represent the skills you perform best. Some of these, however, probably represent skills which you may perform well but do not especially enjoy; you do them only because they have to be done. Some are skills which you enjoy and you do them because they are fun. From the list above, select six Success Factors that are the most important to you and that you enjoy.

1.

____

2.

____

3.____

4.

____

5.

____

6.

____

These are your six **KEY SUCCESS FACTORS**. They are your *motivated* Success Factors because they are the reasons you go to work eagerly every day. They are the six functions you perform the very best and enjoy the most. These are your six most marketable skills and are the main skills you should "sell" to your interviewer.

But, if your six motivated Success Factors are not on your interviewer's list of HIS highest needs, you may as well move on. You may indeed get the job because you're the best prepared for the interview, but chances are good that you won't enjoy the job to the fullest and you'll be looking for another one in short order.

SUCCESS FACTOR WORKSHEET											
Success Factors	**1**	**2**	**3**	**4**	**5**	**6**	**7**	**8**	**9**	**10**	**Total Circled**
Adapted											
Analyzed											
Assisted											
Calculated											
Communicated											
Counseled											
Created/Designed											
Decreased											
Demonstrated											
Developed											
Directed											
Drafted											
Envisioned											
Established											

Estimated											
Evaluated											
Expedited/Facilitated											
Forecasted											
Identified											
Implemented											
Improved											
Increased											
Initiated											
Investigated											
Maintained											
Managed											
Marketed											
Motivated											
Negotiated											
Organized/Planned											
Persuaded											
Prepared											
Presented											
Produced											
Programmed											
Promoted											
Published											
Recommended											
Recruited											
Researched											
Selected											

Solved											
Trained											

Bonus Worksheet 3 – Making Contacts

Who can help you potentially make contact with a decision maker at your desired firm? These aren't people who can help you "find a job", rather they are people who can give you an introduction to your interviewer.

The Friendship Checklist

Family
Spouse's family
Close friends
Builders, plumbers, electricians
Current clients
PTA members
Fellow classmates
Former professors
Parents of your child's friends
Professional societies
Club officers
Hobby groups
Social groups
Executive recruiters
Church groups
Religious leaders
Fraternity/Sorority members
Current or former employers
Fellow employees
Professionals
       Dentist
       Doctor
       Attorney
       CPA
       Financial Planner
       Banker
    Veterinarian

Realtor
Insurance Agent

Fellow vacationers
Former customers, vendors, buyers, sales reps
Librarians
Friends of your spouse
Chamber of Commerce members
Parent's friends
People you meet online
Leaders in other departments

If you haven't spoken with someone for quite some time, it may not be the best idea to launch into a networking speech.

Establish rapport and rebuild those bridges.
Explain your situation.
> *"I was just laid off. The company downsized … "*
> *"I've decided I need more management responsibility … "*
> *"The new chairman and I disagree on the company's future … "*

Tell them what you want.
> *"I want a team environment … "*
> *"I want to use my education and experience to their fullest …"*

Ask for advice and ideas.
> *"Your encouragement has always meant the world to me … "*
> *"I've always counted on you to spark my creativity … "*
> *"Would you mind going over my resume and giving me some feedback?"*

End with a warm, friendly, and enthusiastic closing. Enthusiasm is contagious and it makes it easier for someone to WANT to help you accomplish your goals.

Bonus Worksheet 4 – Handling Business Introductions

First impressions are important and business introductions give you the chance to create a good, long-lasting impression. Make sure to conduct yourself with proper etiquette when you meet someone for the first time, especially in an interview.

When you're introduced in a business setting:

- **Stand up:** If you're seated, it's polite to stand up when you're introduced.
- **Smile:** A smile creates warmth and shows that you're pleased to meet the person. Failing to smile can turn the other person off.
- **Make eye contact:** Making eye contact for the first few seconds of the introduction shows the person you're meeting that you're focused on them and that you consider this introduction important.
- **Shake hands firmly:** A firm handshake communicates professionalism and confidence. The key is your grip. Squeeze firmly and pump up and down two or three times while looking the person in the eye. Don't offer or take just the fingers and don't offer a limp fish either.
- **Make a point of remembering their name:** Unless you expressly make a mental note to remember a name, it'll fly in one ear and right out the other. Repeat their name and say, "It's a pleasure to meet you, [name]."
- **Use titles until told otherwise:** Should you use first names? No, not at first. Whether to use a title (Mr., Ms., Dr., etc.) or call someone by their first name is usually a matter of context. One good rule of thumb is to use the proper title until the other person asks you to do otherwise.
- **Should you introduce yourself?** In an interview you should only introduce yourself at the beginning of the meeting. Otherwise, wait to be introduced to anyone else that may be involved in the interview process. Many companies will parade you around the office to get several other employees first impression. If no one introduces you, it's fine to introduce yourself. The key is not to be too shy or too aggressive

with your own introduction.

If You Forget a Name

Everyone forgets names once in a while. Whatever you do, DON'T forget your interviewer's name. If you forget one, don't make a big deal—simply say, "I'm sorry, I've drawn a blank on your name," make a concerted effort to remember the name this time, and then move on.